Templars

by

John Aquilla Kershaw

authorHOUSE®

AuthorHouse™
1663 Liberty Drive
Bloomington, IN 47403
www.authorhouse.com
Phone: 1-800-839-8640

First published by AuthorHouse 2/01/2011

ISBN: 978-1-4567-2329-3 (sc)
ISBN: 978-1-4567-2320-0 (e)

Printed in the United States of America

PROLOGUE

A missive from the darkness

The mist hung low over the Snake River. As I looked around I saw hieroglyphics, carved in stone by the ancient ones. The spirits of the lowland natives swirled around me. How could I read from those rocks when even the great Chief Joseph couldn't explain those hieroglyphics?

I was dressed all in white as I took my position. John the Baptist questioned his worthiness when Christ came to him for baptism. John said "No, my Lord you should baptize me." Then he baptized the Savior of man. I, like John the Baptist, questioned my worthiness as I stood there in the mist.

I could hear the roar of the rapids of Hells Canyon behind me. The sight of Christ standing in the boat with his hands outstretched came to me as he calmed the Sea of Galilee. It was like He stood there on those rocks and calmed this sacred pool for his salmon to rest in as they got ready to challenge the rapids of Hells Canyon in their circle of life.

I looked to the shore, and you stood there all dressed in white waiting for me to beckon. I glanced at the high priest who had positioned himself to witness full immersion. He smiled. I turned and put my hands out to you. You looked like a Celtic Princess all dressed in white as your feet mingled with the misty water and you floated into my arms as we started our journey to the veil.

You were eight years old and I was sixteen, as I bent over and whispered in your ear, "Sunny, am I worthy to do this holy thing?" You looked up into my eyes and said, "You hold the Priesthood of God and I know your heart is worthy to do this holy thing, now baptize me in these sacred waters of the Lamanites."

I raised my right arm to the square and called on the Father and the Son and the Holy Ghost. My arm came down and I immersed you in the waters just below Hells Canyon. Then I pulled you up to me. You put your arms around my neck and asked that the promise of the Holy Ghost never leave you and that I honor my priesthood forever.

Cancer eats at your body now as my son anoints you with consecrated oil. I lay my hands on your head and ask Father in heaven to remember the promise of the Holy Ghost to comfort you. As our hands rest on your head your hands entwine with ours. There are tears. I call for all the blessings of heaven to come to you. Then the Holy Ghost takes the pain away.

All the clans are there, Sunny, as the veil entwines with the wind. Then you dance to the Celtic moods in the Celestial sphere, as now you have passed through the Veil into Grandpa's arms. Like the day the angels rolled the stone back from the tomb of Christ, the whole earth dances in the Celestial sphere.

DEDICATION

To David O. McKay the prophet
that dedicated my uncle's grave
and at the same time held my aunt
Sadie's hand and blessed our family
Also
Marybeth
Dawn
Helen
Megan
Mimi
Britney
Emily
Rachel
Lisa
Bree
Emita
Raquel
and last but not least my beloved Kathleen

CONTENTS

Sorrow In The Bitterroots

I guess my dad decided that he had to go farther in his search of the answers to the questions he had about this thing called mortality. It seems that's what war doe's to men, when the fighting's done they spend the rest of their lives looking for answers to ques-tions they can't understand. So after we left Union Oregon we caught a train in Portland and didn't get off un-til we got to the big sky country of Montana.

There he got an-other job on a big di-ary farm. I remember that he had to milk one hundred and twenty five head of cows twice a day. I don't know why I remem- ber that, it's just one of those things that stick in my mind

We didn't live on the farm this time, the farmer didn't have enough housing for all of his hired hands. So dad found us a house in town. I can still remember so well all of the neighbors and everyday I still think of the school I went too. I still remember so well that town we lived in 45 years ago.

The dairy processed it's own milk, bottled it and sold it to stores and delivered to peoples homes. My brother and I would get up early in the morning with dad and go out to the dairy with him. He would go into the cooler and get us all a little cold bottle of chocolate milk, man what a treat that was. Then we would go up to the big barn and watch dad as he milked all those cows. My brother and I were always amazed at how each cow seemed to get into the same stall each day. Dad had a name for each one. Is all he had to do was point and the cow he was pointing at would do what he wanted. It was almost like dad would just think what he desired and that's, what they would do. It seemed like dad was a conductor up on a podium and he would wave his hands and the whole herd would move as one, as they filed into their stalls. Then he would play this old record player and milk his cows and gently talk to them, as the sounds of the classics drifted through the barn. One of dad's favorate songs was a classic named Home. I learned later in my life the it came from the Fatom of the Opera.

I would lay up in the hay loft and watch him for hours, I guess it was because I had never seen this side of him before. Now that I look back I believe dad may have started to put that war in the Pacific behind him. As he moved among those cows and at times even sang to them, it seemed like he would change into someone else. Maybe the man he was before he went to war, the man us kids never knew.

Then one day all of our lives began to change and we didn't even know it. We were standing in the corral near the barn when I saw this pretty blond girl running towards us. Dad said that she was the bosses little girl. She jumped up on the fence and with a huge smile, said hi! All summer we played, she showed my brother and I every secret hiding place on that dairy farm. She knew all the cows by name and could ride a horse like she was part of the horses main. One morning she came to the barn real early and found Larry and I watching dad as he conducted his symphony. She never said a word just laid down beside us and looked down at him and listened as he sang the Old Rocking Chair and then turned on the classics. He always told us that the cows gave more milk if they listened to good classical music.

My brother and I both fell in love with that little girl. After a long day of playing she would sneak into the bottling plant and get us all a cold bottle of milk. We would slip off to one of her hiding places and just lay back and drink that wonderful chocolate treat. What a summer that was, but it just ended to soon.

One day my brother and I stayed home to go shopping with mom for school supplies. It was in the early afternoon when dad came home and he looked like the day I saw him walking down the ramp of the Blackball ferry, on Bainbridge Island up in Washington, the day he came home from the war in the Pacific. He wouldn't tell mom what was wrong, he just went out on the back porch to the big easy chair he used to sit in to watch the sunset as it slipped behind the Bitterroot mountains and faded into the western sky.

Mom went next door and used the phone to call the dairy and find out what was wrong. When she came back she was crying real loud, she picked my little sister Anita up and went into her room and closed the door. It was days later that mom finally told us what had happen. Our little girl friend had been playing in the hay loft of the big barn. She was coming down from the upper level and jumped into a hay stack on the lower floor and onto a pitch fork and died.

My dad was the one that found her and blamed himself for not seeing the pitch fork laying there. He wasn't the one who left it there, one of the farm hands had, but he still blamed himself.

Dad sat there on that back porch for weeks, looking out over the fields towards the mountains. It was like he was looking for that pretty little girl to come running up and say hi! Our little girl friends dad (the owner of the dairy farm) sat and talked to dad for days trying to get him to come back to work. He pleaded with dad to please believe that it wasn't his fault, but nothing moved him.

Then one day he just came in off the porch and said he was going to find a job. My father lived to be seventy years old and just before he died we talked about what we had seen in the two different wars we had fought in. The World War two he was in and Viet Nam where my brother and I had served. But he never talked about our little friend and I know that bothered him more than any thing that ever happened in his life.

In the Bitterroot Valley of western Montana there are springs our little friend called desert springs, that come right up out of the ground. My brother and I would be looking for a place to fish and all of a sudden there would be this beautiful clear cold creek coming right up out of the earth. It was just suddenly there and then it would make it's way down through the valley until it disappeared into the Bitterroot River.

It seems to me now as I 'm older and can reflect on the past with a different mind set, that our little girl friend was like those desert springs. She just suddenly appeared into our lives and then tike the little sparkling creeks created by those mysterious desert springs, she just seemed to disappear into eternity.

When I visit my brother Larry three or four times a year, I kneel down beside his bronze headstone and gently drive a little American flag into the ground. I look at his name cast in yellow iron and then my eye's focus on the word (Viet Nam). I believe I may have found part of the answers to the questions my father, brother and I have had about this life. I believe the questions we struggled with for so many years have to be grouped into two parts. The first group is our questions of our own mortality and how easy we can die and that no man is promised another breath,we can die in a second. The second group of questions are questions of morality and how easy it can be to pull the trigger without an after thought, when the madness of war is all around. It seemed that in the madness we went mad too. Then when it was over we were thrown back into the world of the sane. That's when the search for answers to that two part question started. I believe that the answers were so hard to find because we needed to separate them first. The search is over for my father and brother, but I know I'll keep trying to clarify them until the day I pass through the vial.

I now feel at peace, because I believe that my father and brother and our little girl friend are together out there some where in the galaxies. I know my kid brother and she are Chasing Bitterroot desert springs, riding horses, drinking cold chocolate milk and watching dad conduct his symphony's. Most of all I believe their all in a place where nothing or no one can ever hurt them again and that they have found the answers to all their questions.

JACKSON

When I was inducted into the army and we arrived at Fort Ord, California, the guard at the main gate stopped the bus. An army M.P. came aboard and said to the bus driver, "My squad car has broken down on me, could you give me and my prisoner a ride over to the post stockade?"

The bus driver said, "Sure it's only a block or two out of my way."

The M.P. went back to his car and opened the back door. He reached into the car and pulled the prisoner out of the car by his feet. The guy stumbled towards the bus with the M.P. howling at him all the way. This little drama had the attention of every man on the bus. The M.P. made two of the recruits in the front go to the back of the bus. Then the cop pushed the prisoner into the seat and up against the window.

All the way to the stockade the M.P. was screaming at the poor jerk. The more he abused the guy the madder I got. When we got to the stockade the M.P. told the guy to get up, but he refused. The M.P. screamed, "Get up, you jerk, or I'll beat your brains out, you'll wish you had never gone AWOL."

The prisoner had slid down on the floor between the seats. The M.P. became enraged and started to hit the guy with his nightstick. I jumped to my feet and yelled at him to stop. Once I had committed myself I stepped towards him and put my fists up. At first he looked at me in total surprise, then he rushed at me with his nightstick raised above his head.

Then I remembered from a long time past of the time my father had defended himself against a man who had lost control. The move I made seemed to come naturally; as the M.P. swung his nightstick at my head I went low and grasped his right wrist in my left hand, then I wrapped my right arm up behind his forearm. The M.P. let out a terrible scream as I pushed backward as hard as I could. Just before his shoulder broke the prisoner got around in my face and screamed, "It's just an act, stop!"

I let the phony M.P. go and he fell to the floor of the bus.

The prisoner said, "We do this just to make you new recruits never go AWOL and end up in this stinking stockade. The army drafts a lot of men who never adjust to military life and this is where they end up, are you one of those men, Maggot!"

I sat down and said, "I thought it was real. I'm sorry, sir."

The phony prisoner got right in my face and said, "You will pay for this, Maggot."

"Who are you, sir?" I ask.

"You'll find out in the morning, now everyone sit down."

As the phony prisoner helped the phony M.P. up from the floor he said, "I think you broke his arm."

I can remember the sinking feeling in my stomach as they

led the man off the bus into the post hospital. Why couldn't I just keep my nose out of things that didn't pertain to me? I was always doing that; it was the story of my life.

I was awake all night worrying about what was going to happen to me in the morning. I had no idea it had been an act. It had to be one of the dumbest things I had ever seen. But it wouldn't be the last dumb thing I saw in the seven years I served my country.

The next morning my friend Luke opened his big mouth in the mess hall. We were eating breakfast, and this black fellow set down with us. While we were talking I told Luke that I heard we would be assigned to A Company 3rd Battalion, and that the first sergeant for that company was said to be the meanest jerk in the army.

"You're crazier than a pet coon, I heard it was B Company of the Fourth Battalion," Luke answered.

I saw it coming, but Luke didn't; the black guy jumped to is feet and shot his best shot right at the tip of Luke's chin. He went head over heels backward and landed on top of the upside down chair and just lay there sound asleep.

The black kid turned to me and asked, "Do you want some of the same, white boy?"

I replied, "No he deserved it, if I thought you were wrong I would have stuck my fork in your ear."

We both looked down at Luke, and my new friend said, "Should be careful who you hang out with. A dummy like that could get you hurt."

I said, "I think he is learning."

"I don't know, man, he looks real stupid to me."

As we stood there looking down at Luke I replied, "I think you my have broken his jaw. He doesn't always look that dumb."

"Hey, you're the guy that almost broke that phony M.P.'s arm last night. What are they going to do to you?"

"I don't know, man, but I don't think they can do anything to me legally. I mean nothing they were doing could have been authorized by the army. It was one of the goofiest things I've ever seen."

We left Luke lying there on the floor of the mess hall and walked back up to the reception center barracks. As we were walking up to the steps of the barracks an orderly asked me if I was the guy that had twisted the first sergeant's arm off last night.

I said, "Yes, sir, but I didn't mean to."

"Don't call me, sir, I work for a living, just get your tail over to the orderly room. The first pig wants to see you."

I looked at my new friend and he just rolled his eyes back and shrugged his shoulders. I thought about running but I didn't know which way to go; they had M.P.s at the front gate and I didn't know where the back gate was. Besides, they more than likely had M.P.s at the back gate too. So I just sucked it up and did what I was told to do.

I knocked on the door of the orderly room, and a booming voice said, "Come in, worm." I opened the door and stepped into hell. The first soldier was standing in front of his desk with his right arm in a sling. The guy that had played the prisoner was walking out of an office behind the first sergeant's desk. When he stepped up by the desk I could see the gold bars of a second lieutenant on his shirt collar.

The first sergeant said, "I brought you here to tell you that we are never going to perform that stupid little skit again. So if you call your Mommy and tell her what happened you'll know that the official story is that I fell down, do you get the drift, worm?"

I stood there for a long moment and then it hit me and I said, "Yes, sergeant."

The first sergeant went on. "I also want to introduce you to your first sergeant for the next eight weeks."

The biggest, meanest looking man I had ever seen stood up from a chair in the corner of the room and slowly walked around the desk and stood right in front of me. I wanted to run but I just stood there ramrod stiff.

"My name is Sergeant Jackson. I hear you are real tough, Maggot."

"No, sir," I said in a weak voice.

Slowly he paced back and forth in front of me and said, "Go back to your barracks—you'll be mine soon enough."

I almost ripped the door off the place as I made my way back into the world. I thanked the Lord for sparing my worthless soul. My new first sergeant was the meanest man I had ever rubbed noses with. I could see the toughness in his eyes but most of all I saw something else: I saw control. That was what I wanted too, but I wasn't sure how to achieve it. Maybe if I watched that old coot long enough I could learn something from him.

As I stood there at the bottom of the orderly room stairs trying to figure out which barracks was mine, I could swear I heard laughter coming from behind the door of that orderly room.

MAGGOT

It didn't take long for Sergeant Jackson to start teaching me self-control. The day after we were sent up the hill to our basic training company the first pig gave me a visit. He walked into the barracks at 9 p.m., and the whole platoon headed for the other end of the building, except me. I was sitting on my footlocker intently trying to make a pair of black combat boots shine when I noticed two legs inside two spit-shined jump boots standing in front of my face.

"Stand up, Maggot!" he screamed.

I jumped up and he put his face about an inch from mine and said, "I have good news for you, Maggot: for the entire eight weeks of basic training you will be on permanent fire watch and KP (kitchen police). You will pull fire watch here in your own barracks from 0200 until 0400 hours. Then you will report to the mess hall and clean pots and pans and grease traps until your platoon moves out for training exercises."

I found my tongue and said, "But, Sarge, I'll never get any sleep, besides I never hurt that first sergeant that bad."

He pulled me even closer to his face and said, "Don't ever

call me Sarge again, do you understand, Maggot? You call me sir."

I worked up as much courage as I could and said, "Yes, sir."

He coldly said, "The swelling in my friend's shoulder was down enough for them to take a good X-ray today, and the ball of the bone that goes into the socket is broken. They operated on him this morning, so don't say you didn't hurt him that bad."

I said the only thing I could think to say: "I'm sorry, sir, I didn't think."

My face was so close to his I couldn't focus on his eyes, as he said, "Remember one thing, Maggot, you aren't paid to think."

He glanced down at my scriptures lying on my footlocker and said, "Give your soul to your Mormon God, Maggot, because your tail belongs to me."

I called Mom the next weekend and told her what they were doing to me and that I wanted to come home. She listened really quietly then said, "I'm sorry, son, but I have already given your bed to your brother. The army is your home now. I'm sorry, Johnny, but you quit high school and joined the army for three years, and I want you to finish your commitment. This is one thing you can't quit. Don't you dare disgrace this family, son, or I promise you I'll pull out every hair on your head."

"They cut all my hair off too, Mom." Then we both started laughing.

She went on. "I know you can do anything they tell you to do, son. Just turn to the Lord when you think you can't take another step."

Then with all my heart I said something I never said enough: "I love you, Mom."

"I love you too, son, good night."

I set there in the phone booth needing someone who would give me a little sympathy. Without thinking I called the wrong person; I called Grandpa.

As I listen to the phone ring I tried to think of what I would say, and then his familiar voice came on the line.

And I said, "Hi, Grandpa, this is Johnny."

"Hi son are you a general yet?"

"No, sir, but I'm in a lot of trouble."

He thought for a moment and then said, "Are you in the stockade?"

I said, "No." Then I told him my long, sad story and waited for his response.

"That's it?" He asked.

"Yes," I said back.

Then he told me, "It sounds like they have you real busy, son. That's what we wanted, right? Call me next weekend during the day. Good night, son."

"Good night, Grandpa. I love you."

"I love you too, son, if you get down, read Moroni 8:3 and think of me."

I said back, "Grandpa, if your Catholic priest catches you reading my Book of Mormon every day, he's going to be hot."

"It's not the priest I'm worried about, he will forgive me—it's your Irish Grandmother that I fear."

"Good night again, Grandpa."

Then he responded before I could hang up the phone. "I'm already pulling strings with a senator here in Oregon so I can pin those silver jump wings on your chest, son. But first you have to get through basic training and jump school. Good night."

I went back to my barracks and took my Book of Mormon from my footlocker. It was late and almost time for me to go on fire watch so I went downstairs and outside to the furnace room. I took a seat on the old iron folding chair we had set up beside the nice warm furnace and leafed through the pages of Moroni until I found 8:3. I sat there in the dim light and let my eyes scan the words of Moroni and thought of Grandpa as I read.

> *I'm mindful of you always in my prayers,*
> *continually praying unto God the Father in*
> *the name of his Holy child, Jesus, That he,*
> *through his infinite goodness and grace, will*
> *keep you through the endurance of faith on*
> *his name to the end.*

I looked up from my scriptures; the first soldier was standing there looking at me. I quickly jumped to my feet.

He leaned into my face and almost whispered, "You have five minutes before your watch starts, Maggot."

"Yes, sir." I whispered back. It was like we didn't want to wake anybody up. I couldn't figure out what he was doing there in the middle of the night. I put my scriptures down on my chair and started my rounds.

But he called me back and got right in my face again and said, "I don't mind you sitting in that nice warm chair and reading now and then, but if I ever catch you sleeping I'll court marshal you. You can do pull-ups on that pull-up bar over there or pushups, whatever you have to do to stay awake. But if I ever catch you so much as cat napping, you'll be mine. Do you understand, Maggot?"

I could hardly speak I was so mad. But something told me, that was what he wanted—besides I wasn't sure I could whip the old man. No matter, how could I let Mom and Grandpa down? So I whispered back, "Yes, sir."

When I came back from doing my rounds he was gone, so I sat down to read my scriptures. It wasn't long before I felt really sleepy so I left that nice, warm furnace room and looked around. I couldn't help wondering if he was watching me. I walked over to the pull-up bar and did as many pull-ups as I could and then dropped to the ground and did twenty pushups. That only made me more tired, and I knew if I went back into that furnace room I would fall asleep.

So I did my rounds and came back to the pull-up bar again and did as many as I could. That went on for almost an hour and when I couldn't lift my arms anymore I walked around the barracks and let the cold night breeze coming off the Pacific Ocean keep me awake.

It was a blessing when my relief came and I went to the mess hall to start my K.P. The smell of breakfast cooking seemed to put new life into my body. I was cleaning the grease trap under the sink when I saw a set of spit-shined jump boots standing there like they had eyes and were watching me. I never looked up I just acted like I didn't see them, and they finally disappeared just like they had appeared.

That went on every day, and I wasn't sure how long I could last. The only day we had off was Sunday, and all I did was sleep and go to church.

I was in the army about two weeks when my company was ushered into a large auditorium. They told us that it was some kind of recruitment pitch for volunteers for the paratroopers. As we waited I sat there having second thoughts of being a trooper, all because of what I was going through in the regular army. They had told us that it was an elite unit and really tough. Maybe I wasn't made for it.

We were all getting restless when all of a sudden the doors behind us flew open and slammed against the wall. Standing there in the doorway was a very strong looking young buck sergeant. As he half walked and half ran down the aisle between the seats I could see the paratroopers' silver jump wings pinned to his chest. The next thing I saw was the paratrooper patch on his cap. Then the patch on his left shoulder. It had the white head of a bald eagle on it, the symbol of the 101st Airborne's screaming eagles.

He stopped in front of us and jumped flat-footed to the hardwood floor of the stage above him. The young trooper landed on the balls of his feet and turned to face us. He just stood there staring out at us; it seemed like he was looking each one of us right in the eyes.

With a booming voice he said, "I'm here looking for men that have guts of steel. Men that can jump behind enemy lines to fight and die alone if that's what it takes to defend the greatest nation on this earth. It's paratroopers I want, men that free-fall with the eagles.

Well there I was. I had told Grandpa I wanted to be a paratrooper, and he believed me. Now I had to make up my mind.

Then I saw the first sergeant standing to the side of curtains of the stage, and he was looking right at me with those steel blue eyes of his. The young paratrooper jumped from the stage and said, "I'll be out in the lobby to sign up any man that thinks he can jump out of the morning sunrise and fight with the first show of light."

About ten men stood and followed this young warrior to the lobby. As I stood to follow I could hear Grandpa's voice telling me that he would be there to pin my silver wings on my chest.

Luke grabbed my arm and said, "Are you nuts?"

"Yes, I am, Luke. I can't explain it right now but we'll talk about it tonight."

I pulled away from Luke's grasp and followed the other men to the lobby. The closer I got to the table where the young sergeant sat I knew I wanted to wear the same silver wings that this mad man wore. I knew I would serve with pride and honor, and most of all I promised myself that I would not shame the name my fathers had given me. Once I reached that table and signed I knew I would never quit.

I was the last man to sign and the last to take my place back in formation as we were about to be herded to are next destination. Then I heard a familiar voice boom out, "Maggot, front and center."

I obeyed and quickly ran and stood before the first soldier and said, "Yes, sir."

Then he said, "Take the guide arm and take your place at the head of the company."

"The guide arm, sir?" I asked

"The pole with the little flag on it," He barked back.

I knew what he meant but I couldn't believe that he wanted me to carry it. I was so tired I didn't think I could carry another ounce without falling on my face. But I turned and re-slung my rifle strap across my chest and my M-1 across my back and took my new position at the head of the company with the guide arm held high and waited for his command to march. But he didn't tell us to march; he told us to double-time. We hadn't gone a hundred yards when I heard him yell, "Pick it up, Maggot."

So I lengthened my stride and dreamed of how nice my

bunk was going to feel that night for the few hours I would be in it. Every time I slowed down I heard his voice from behind, saying, "Pick it up, Maggot."

A couple of weeks later we were guided back to the barracks earlier than we normally did. I couldn't believe it we were going to get off early, and I could almost feel that bunk under my back. But just before we broke ranks the first sergeant told us the bad news. We were told to eat supper and be ready to load up on trucks to go to the night firing range at 2000 hours. So I ate supper as fast as I could and went and lay down to get as much sleep as I could since I knew it was going to be a long night.

They loaded us up in long semi-trucks like cattle and made our way to the night firing range. I remember thinking that at least we didn't have to double-time the ten miles. When we got there I tried to hide behind the rest of the company. The range was lit up when we first got there. But it was just dark enough that I thought I could keep out off the sight of the first soldier. I can't believe I was so stupid, because everywhere I went I had that guide arm. I couldn't even go to the latrine without him knowing where I was. If I tried to lower it even for a few moments, it would bring the first sergeant's bark: "Hold that guide arm up, Maggot."

So there I was in the back of the company trying to hide when I heard the words, "Maggot, front and center."

I ran out to the front of the company and stopped in front of the first sergeant. "You qualified expert with that old M-1 of yours. Now we are going to see how good you really are. You and I are going to stand in that foxhole over there and shoot at targets on those hills behind us."

I glanced over his shoulder, and all I could see was

blackness. Then he said, "Have you ever shot Rattle Battle, Maggot?"

I answered, "No, sir."

"Those hills behind me are going to be lit up with spot lights, and we'll see targets about two hundred to five hundred yards out. Normally we would have eighty rounds apiece and have one minute to fire all eighty rounds, but tonight you and I will have one hundred and sixty rounds and forty-five seconds to shoot them all. It won't matter if we hit the targets—we just have to get close. All one hundred and sixty rounds will be tracer rounds, so the platoon sergeants standing behind us can see how close we get. But the most important thing is who shoots all his rounds off first, because if I beat you there will be two more extra hours of fire watch for you tonight. Do you understand, Maggot?"

"Yes, sir," I yelled back.

I walked over to the foxhole and drove the pole of the guide arm into a pile of dirt just behind the foxhole and jumped down into the hole and waited for the first sergeant.

I took my place at the left side of the foxhole and laid all one hundred and sixty M-1 rounds in front of me where they would be easy to reach when I reloaded. Then from behind me came, "Move to the right side, Maggot."

I couldn't figure the difference but I moved. I realized then that my ammo would be closer to my right hand when I was re-loading. Then I really couldn't figure why he wanted the left side, but I was sure I would know soon enough.

Then the range officer bellowed out, "Lock and load."

I jammed my first clip into my rifle and waited for the order to fire. Then the spotlights came on, the first targets jumped up, and the range officer screamed into his loudspeakers, "Fire!"

Then I found out why the first pig wanted the left side. You see when an M-1 rifle is fired it ejects its empty bullet casing to the right and whoever dug the foxhole had dug it so we were really close. When the first soldier fired his rifle the hot, empty casing would hit me in the head, neck, and back. He had moved over closer to me, and it seemed he was aiming the casings at me as he fired. Some of them hit me in the neck and rolled down the back of my shirt, burning me all the way to my belt. I knew that he was doing it to slow me down but it only made me mad, and I believe it made me faster. I completely shut out the pain, and as fast as that old M-1 could fire and reload I pulled the trigger. When the empty clip would fly out I would jam another one into the breach of the rifle almost before the empty clip could hit the ground.

The forty-five seconds seemed like it would never end, but before I knew it I was out of ammo and the first soldier was still firing. I beat him by about five seconds. When it was all over I dared not look at him; I just waited until the range officer cleared us, and then I jumped up out of the two-man foxhole, took my guide arm, and took my place at the back of the company. That was when I noticed that all the other foxholes were one-man foxholes and I realized that the two-man hole had just been dug for me and the first soldier.

As the other men started taking their places on the firing line, I heard a familiar whisper behind me. "Don't smile, Maggot." I just bowed my head.

Then he got really close to my ear so no one else could hear and said, "Don't bow your head to me, Maggot. You're an American soldier—we don't bow our heads to anyone except God."

I whispered back, "I wasn't bowing to you, First Sergeant.

I was asking Heavenly Father to give me the strength not to try to kick your tail."

For the first time I saw a twinkle in his eyes, and he turned and walked away from me.

The last day of basic training finally came. I had my orders to go to medical school at Fort Sam Houston, Texas. When I finished my sixteen weeks of medical school at Fort Sam I was to go to Fort Bragg to attend jump school and become a paratrooper.

They told me I would be with the last troopers to go through jump school at Bragg. Then it would close down, and from then on everyone would go to Fort Benning for jump school.

I had one more night of fire watch. At 0200 I relieved the man before me. I put some coal in the old furnace so there would be plenty of hot water for the troops in the morning and to take the chill off of the cold sea breeze moving in from the Pacific Ocean. Then I made my rounds through the barracks.

I caught one guy on the second floor smoking in bed. I told him, "I will report you to the CQ if you don't put that cigarette out and leave it out. These old wooden barracks burn like cedar kindling when they catch fire."

He replied, "Jump out the window, jerk."

I started to write his name down and what time it was. Then I was going to the orderly room and report him. Everyone in the barracks was in danger. I told him what I was going to do but that I would give him one more chance. He laughed at me and then swallowed the cigarette.

"Now are you happy, mister permanent fire watch?" he replied as he smiled at me with a toothless grin—the product of a fight he was in two or three weeks before.

"I hope it burns you all the way to your tail, Maggot," I answered.

When I went downstairs I could hear him running to the water fountain. I couldn't believe some of the people the army let in. But I guessed they knew better than I did.

I finished my rounds and went back to the furnace room to write a letter to Grandpa and read my scriptures. I was half into the letter when the door slowly opened. There stood the first soldier.

"Sit, Private," he said as I started to jump to my feet.

I couldn't believe it—that was the first time he hadn't called me a maggot. He reached over and pulled an old metal bucket out from behind the boiler and sat where he could warm his hands against the warm metal. I waited for him to say something.

"I went to jump school almost twenty years ago. I jumped Normandy and Korea. What a time we had, I wish I could go with you, son," he said in a low voice.

We talked through the night, and I told him of my father and how bitter he was when he came back from the war in the Pacific. I told him of my mother, who would give me anything she had in this world. Then I told him of my grandfather, the greatest man I ever knew.

And then as the day began to dawn, he said, "Some great man once said that the eyes are the windows of the soul. I saw fire in your soul, son, and in the last eight weeks I have tried to put a little water on that fire."

As he stood he reached into his shirt pocket and pulled out a little brown copy of the Book of Mormon so I could see it and said, "Always keep this near your heart, son."

I was dumbfounded as I said, "You are a Mormon, sir?"

He answered, "I was born under the covenant, son.

Never forget you're a soldier of Helaman; never give up. And remember the covenant you made when you entered the waters of baptism is your refuge from the storms of this world."

I still remember the smell of his breath.

SILVER WINGS

My first day in jump school was like no other I had ever experienced. I got off the shuttle bus where I would make my home for the next three weeks. I had just thrown my duffle bag up on my shoulder and headed towards the orderly room the bus driver had pointed out. Before I got three steps, I heard this booming voice behind me.

"Hey you, leg."

I turned to look, and there stood Sergeant Jackson's twin brother, only his name tag said, "Richards."

He yelled at me, "What do you have on your head, Maggot?"

I thought, *Oh Lord, I'm still a maggot. Please give me a break and a little self-control.* Then, I said, "My hat, sir."

"Hat!" He screamed in my face, "That's not a hat. It looks like a flying saucer. This is a hat." He pointed at the little green hat that looked like a large knife blade sitting on top of his crew cut.

I almost whispered, "Oh, my garrison cap, it's in my duffle bag, sir."

"Well, get it out of your duffle bag, leg, and stop whispering," he screamed. I later found out 'leg' was what paratroopers call anyone who's not a paratrooper.

I had put my garrison cap all the way to the bottom of my duffle bag. Now garrison cap isn't exactly what he called this piece of headgear. He had a slang word for it that is not made for the ears of a missionary. I had put my garrison cap all the way to the bottom of my duffle bag, so I took all my clothes out of my bag to get to it and put it on my head. I gently laid my round service cap, with its spit-shined bill on the sidewalk next to my duffle bag, like he told me to.

It was during the third summer I stayed with Grandpa when I realized how strong a desire it was for him to win when he set up his chessboard. I talked to my cousins about it, and they knew of no one in the family who had ever beaten him: in fact we didn't know anyone in La Grande, Oregon, who had ever defeated him at chess.

Some may say that beating kids all the time isn't the way to teach them how to play a game like chess. But Grandpa didn't just teach us how to play chess; he taught us the history that shaped the world we lived in and all its wonders. Anyone who thinks he didn't teach my brother and I the right way, well, all they have to do is place a chessboard in front of one of us and pick their king and we will shortly teach them the correct way to pronounce the word 'checkmate.'

I couldn't wait for the day to end so I could sit on Grandpa's front porch. I would daydream of being at that chessboard and going to some distant land to defend my king. We always had a different kingdom to defend. One night it was the Zulu King who defeated the British Royal 24th Infantry in the first battle of the Zulu War of 1878. Grandpa was a British General and I was a Zulu prince. What a war it was, but in the end Grandpa checkmated my Zulu King and I bowed before the British throne.

The next night I might have been Bluebeard the legendary knight who rode beside Joan of Arc as she rode to a flaming death at the stake, while she fought to set some spineless aristocrat on the throne of France. But in the end I always heard my grandpa's Irish laugh and the word 'checkmate.'

My grandfather was a true master of history and of teaching little kids how to dream. The thing I dreamed of most of all was checkmating that old man who taught me how to dream.

I'll never forget the night I chose to defend King Edward the first of England. Grandpa had the choice of defending Wales or Scotland; he chose to be a Scottish chieftain. Edward the First had waged war against his northern neighbors for decades.

Grandpa said to me, "Edward the First was the great-grandfather of the ruthless Black knight, which is another story. Tomorrow night we will speak of Edward the First and how he spent his whole life trying to unite the British Isles and initiated the principle that only Parliament should change the law. This will be a good lesson for you, Johnny my boy, because you have Irish, Welsh, Scottish, and English blood flowing through your veins. Oh! There's a little Shawnee Indian mixed in there too."

Then Grandpa stood up from his chair, handed me a book and said, "This is the history of the warrior king you must defend tomorrow night. I'll be one of the Scottish chieftains who defended his king to the death. Read it well, son and be ready to defend your rotten English king."

I stood, took the book and said, "I will, sir. I'll defend him until the last breath leaves my body. I'll be Sir Reed, the Earl of Norfolk, who rode at his side as they tried to defeat Scotland for the third time, King Edward's last attempt before his death."

As I looked into his smiling, Irish eyes he put his arm around my shoulder and said, "You have been reading this book behind my back haven't you, son? Goodnight, laddie."

I read the book until late into the night and early the next morning. When we took our breaks from bucking hay the next day in the hay fields of the Grande Ronde Valley, I would pull the book out of my lunchbox and read.

The other teenagers on the crew teased me about being in the old Irishman's summer school. But I could tell by the way they said it that they wished they could be on that front porch with us. I never invited them because that was my time with the old dragoon as we rode to the four corners of the earth to defend our kings.

I had a strange feeling that I was finally close to checkmating the old man. I waged two campaigns against the Scottish king that night, but his chieftain warrior kept me in check.

When I heard the word 'checkmate' for the second time I asked Grandpa if I could attack Wales and would he defend it. He said he would. So the Welsh and English took their places. The battle was fierce, and it was written in the pages of history that I should have won, but somehow Grandpa did what he always did: he checkmated me with that big Irish smile said, "Checkmate, laddie."

So we turned back to the north and the Scots once again. It was the bloodiest of the three wars my King fought against the Scottish king and his chieftains. As I retreated back into England and with most of my army destroyed, I left my king's right flank unguarded. Then I heard the familiar words coming from those smiling Irish lips: "Checkmate, Johnny my boy."

That night when the carved ivory armies were put to rest, Grandpa said to me, "Tomorrow night I will be a Roman centurion, and Pontius Pilot will be my King and the Pharisees will be my army." He laid a new testament in my lap and said,

"Get ready to defend your king, the Lord Jesus Christ, Johnny my boy."

I sat there looking down at the scriptures in my lap and wondered how I could ever defend this humble king of the Jews. I knew my Grandfather could quote from memory almost every verse written on its pages, and he knew every step my king the Lord Jesus Christ took on his trip to the cross.

I stood up from my chair just as Grandpa was going through the front door, and I said to him, "Goodnight, Grandpa. Be ready to defend your cowardly king and his deceitful army."

He stopped and looked back at me and without an Irish smile on his lips said, "I'll be ready, Johnny my boy."

As I lay in my bed and started to read, I could hear Grandpa already snoring downstairs and I knew he was ready. When I started to read my scriptures I began to remember all of my Sunday school teachers who had spent so much of their lives trying to teach me what was written on those pages. I thought of all the early, cold mornings as I scripture-chased in seminary while Grandpa's other Catholic grandchildren slept warm in their beds.

Then I realized that Grandpa may have picked the wrong king to defend. Because when my Sunday school and seminary teachers thought I was sleeping, I was only trying to visualize what my Brother Jesus and our Heavenly Father must have gone through as the drama on Calvary hill took its course.

After just a few verses I realized I didn't need to read the whole New Testament. The biggest part about playing chess with Grandpa was that you had to justify each move you made with historical fact, or in the case of the New Testament, verse. If you made a mistake in your move it still counted, but your fact or verse had to make sense. In all my scripture-chasing I had written all the verses that had been clear to me in the margins of the pages. So now all I had to do was play a good game of chess. I reached down into my suitcase, laid my hand on my marked and worn scriptures and dreamed of checking the old man who taught me how to dream.

I said my prayers for the first time in a long time and thanked the Lord for all the good Sunday school teachers he had given me over the years. I rolled over, went to sleep and dreamed of checkmating Grandpa as we battled throughout the Holy Land.

I thought about how I would defend the Lord Jesus all day as I threw bales of hay onto the conveyor belt that took them to the top of the stack of hay on the truck. This time I would fight with my soul instead of a sword. I wasn't sure I could defend Jesus Christ, but I knew if I wasn't ready now I never would be.

That evening as we ate supper, I caught Grandpa looking out of the side of his eyes at me. I knew he had been thinking about the game too. My family was the only Mormons in Grandpa's clan, and he tried really hard to prove that his Irish Catholic religion was the only right one on this earth. I had a feeling this was going to be more than just a chess game this night.

I found I was right as for the first time Grandpa set a clock beside the black ebony chessboard and said, "Each move must be made within fifteen minutes and backed up with a verse from the Bible, not the book of Mormon."

It seemed that the scriptures became clearer than they had ever been to me as we justified each of our moves with the verse we picked. As the stars got brighter and the moon moved over Grandpa's front porch, we waged our holy war back and forth across the sacred lands of Abraham.

Then Grandpa noticed my old, worn scriptures. He reached across the little table and picked them up, then laid them back down without a word.

Then out of nowhere the old dragoon checked my Lord with a Roman centurion. I then moved the Apostle Paul in between the Roman and my Lord. If the Roman centurion had taken Paul, then Peter would have taken him and put Pontius Pilate in check. Pontius Pilate and the chief priests smelled victory.

As Grandpa concentrated on moving one of his centurions up to flank the other side of my Lord, he made a mistake I never thought I would see him make. I sat there quietly and listened as Grandpa read his verse supporting his move.

When he was done I set the clock and took my whole fifteen minutes to make sure that crafty old Irishman had not set a trap. Just before the bell rang on the clock telling me my time was up, I moved my Queen Mary, mother of my king and Lord Jesus Christ, directly in front of the Roman Governor Pontius Pilate and said, "Checkmate, your majesty."

Then Grandpa's eyes moved from the chessboard up to my eyes, and with that sparkling Irish smile he said, "You have won, Johnny my boy, but that's not the way it really happened, laddie. Your Lord was checkmated on Calvary. Look through the window above my chair where that crucifix hangs. They drove nails through his hands and feet, and a Roman Centurion drove a spear through his chest."

Then as he sat there looking into my eyes it seemed as if his blue Irish eyes turned to gray and he went on, "Then he died."

I then summoned up all of the courage I had and said, "No, Grandpa, no one ever checkmated the Lord Jesus Christ. They checked him and hurt him real bad, Grandpa. I think Heavenly Father must have hid in some far-off universe so he couldn't see what they did to his only begotten son. But they never checkmated him, because he was lifted up into heaven by our Heavenly Father, and he leads my church today."

He sat there looking at me for the longest time and slowly

placed the little ivory soldiers in their box as I read the verse I felt justified my point of view. Then he stood and said, "Let's sit awhile."

He put his big arm around my shoulders as we walked over to his porch swing. We sat and silently watched the sparks from the sawmill's stack that sat behind his farm as we slowly swung back and forth. The heat from the mill's incinerator was so intense that it would blow the sparks high into the sky, and it looked like they would mingle with the stars.

I said, "I'm going to join the army after this next year of school is done. I want to be a paratrooper, and I want you there to pin my silver wings on my chest."

And Grandpa said, "I'll pin them on if they will let me, Johnny my boy."

Then Grandpa asked, "Can you see well enough in this light to read two more verses?"

I said, "Yes," and he asked me to repeat the verse I had used to support the move that had checkmated him.

So I read St. Matthew 28:7: "And go quickly, and tell his disciples that he is risen from the dead; and, behold he goeth before you to Galilee; there shall ye see him; lo, I have told you."

Grandpa said, "You were right, lad; this verse justified the move. Now read me one more verse, then it's to bed for us, read the eighth Psalm 3-5."

So I read: "When I consider thy heavens, the work of thy fingers, the moon and the stars, which thou hast ordained; what is man, that thou art mindful of him? And the Son of man, that thou visited him? For thou hast made him a little lower than the angels, and hast crowned him with glory and honor."

I asked Grandpa if I could ask one more question before we went to bed.

"What is it, Johnny?" he almost whispered.

I said, "How could you, Dad, and my uncles be brave enough to serve in a war? Grandma said you were all too gentle to do such a terrible thing."

Grandpa thought for what seemed a long time and then asked, "Do you have your Book of Mormon?"

I said, "Yes." Then he told me to turn to Alma Chapter 56:47.

I was stunned. "Grandpa, have you read the Book of Mormon?"

He answered, "Johnny, your Joseph Smith was a great man, and I believe God may have been talking to him now and then. Correct me if I misquote this verse; I believe it's the answer to your question—follow along, Lad. Alma 56:47, Now they had never fought, yet they did not fear death; and they did think more upon the liberty of their Fathers than they did upon their lives; yea, they had been taught by their Mothers, that if they did not doubt, God would deliver them."

I was amazed that my Grandfather could recite word for word a verse from the Book of Mormon. It was the answer to a question I had since my uncle had come back from WW 2 only to take his own life. I had read the story of the stippling warriors of Helaman's army but I didn't remember that verse until then.

I moved over next to Grandpa and asked him, "You are a Catholic, and you have always questioned my beliefs. Why would you read the Book of Mormon?"

He looked deep into my eyes and said, "Because you gave me the Book of Mormon your mother gave you when you were baptized and ask me to read it. I couldn't say no to you, laddie."

"Grandpa, do you still have my Book of Mormon?"

"Yes, son, and I read it every day, but don't ever tell your grandmother—it would kill her if she knew."

My grandfather was the greatest man I ever knew. I never told anyone about the Book of Mormon he had with my name inscribed on it. I know I checkmated that old man whom I loved so in a game. But no one ever checkmated him in the game of life, any more then my Lord Jesus Christ was checkmated. I know with all my soul that he has since stepped right up there with the angels that he spent his life looking up at.

I then quickly repacked my bag while this new sergeant screamed at me, "You looked like a bus driver with that flying saucer on your head, leg."

Then he told me, "Now, leg, put your duffle bag on top of your shoulders, across the back of your neck, and hold it with both hands."

By this time we had drawn a crowd of about a half dozen sergeants that all looked just like my tormentor. I knew he was leading up to something, so I just stood there with my duffle bag across my shoulders and waited for his next order.

"Can you do squats, leg?" he bellowed at me.

"Yes, sir," I bellowed back.

With his teeth shining in my eyes, he said, "Good. Now stand on that flying saucer you call a hat and give me a hundred squats."

Why hadn't someone told me that the only hat a paratrooper wore was a garrison cap? I couldn't believe my ears. I was hardly able to do a hundred squats without my duffle bag on my shoulders. I did what I was told and could feel the shining bill on my service cap crumble beneath my weight.

At thirty squats he said with half a laugh, "Hurry up, leg, I don't have all day."

At fifty squats it felt like my legs were on fire and they were made of Jell-O, and spasms were building up in my shoulders from holding the duffle bag. At sixty, I thought I was going to die as my sixty-pound duffle bag pushed me towards the ground. At seventy, I couldn't go back up. It felt like I was frozen in the fetal position. Then I fell over, and the weight of the duffle bag drove my nose into the grass and dirt next to the sidewalk.

In a more calm voice, he said, "Not too bad, leg. The last guy only did sixty." Then he got real close and whispered, "Sergeant Jackson called me six weeks ago and told me you were coming. Pull my dog chain and read my name on my dog tag and never forget my name. Then read the bottom of my tag."

My eyes went from Richards down to LDS, and all I could think was N*o, Lord, not another soldier of Helaman, another spear catcher.*

Then he whispered, "Don't you ever give up. Now report to the orderly room and clean the grass stains off of your nose."

Before I turned away I said, "I'll die in your arms before I give up."

Then the sergeant standing next to him asked, "Why do you treat these Mormon legs harder than the others?"

I strained to hear what he whispered back. "Someday I'll tell you a story of two brothers named Joseph and Hyrum and then maybe you'll understand."

As the other sergeant pulled his wallet out he said, "I didn't think this chubby sucker could do fifty."

Then with the strap of my duffle bag held tightly I asked, "Are you my First Sergeant?"

"No, leg, I'm your jump master, and that's even worse," he answered with a smile.

This same man taught me how to jump from an airplane over the next three weeks. But most of all he inspired me. He instilled in my heart that I could jump behind enemy lines to fight and die alone if I had to. I began to believe that my country was a living thing and that we were the vital organs that gave it life. I grew to believe that when that living thing needed to be protected I had to be ready. Like my father before me, I learned that this country was bigger than all my dreams.

But it wasn't easy for me as Mother Nature had given me the shaft. She seemed to have left some muscles out of my shoulders, or I just never developed them the way I should have. Because of this pull-ups were very hard for me to do. When everyone was done for the evening, I was outside the barracks struggling to touch my chin on the pull-up bar. I just made the minimum count the day before I graduated.

There had been days I wanted to quit, but Grandpa kept telling me in his letters that he and my uncles were going to drive out for my graduation. Three thousand miles they were going to drive in Grandpa's new Buick Road Master. He said he wanted to break it in. I was so glad I kept going.

At the awards ceremony all the new paratroopers in my class stood in ranks waiting to receive our silver cherry jump wings. Mom told me on the phone the night before that Grandpa had talked my father into coming with him. What would I say to the man who had walked out of my life four years before? It had been four years since my mom and dad had separated. Four years since I had heard my father cry, the marine I didn't think could cry.

My emotions ran high as I searched the grandstands for my family. Then I saw them, my father and uncles, but I didn't see Grandpa, and my heart skipped a beat. Was he OK? Had the trip been too much for him?

As we stood there at parade rest, I saw something red out

of the side of my eyes. I turned my head ever so slightly, and there stood the old Royal British Northern Dragoon in his red British uniform. There were a dozen little kids standing around him asking questions.

My commanding officer called us to attention, and then we did an about face and saluted as the colors were presented. Then the regimental bagpipe band from the 82nd Airborne struck up a military march. Grandpa stepped out from beside the bleachers and, in time to bagpipes, walked across the parade grounds. He stopped in front of my C.O. and saluted. My C.O. saluted back and then stepped up beside Grandpa. He did an about face, then barked out my name and said, "Front and center."

I was stunned. The old Dragoon had pulled enough strings with that senator he knew on the Ways and Means Committee, and they were going to let this magnificent old man in his red uniform pin my silver wings on my chest. I wasn't expecting this. I thought that Grandpa was just spinning one of his Irish yarns when he said he was going to try to pin my silver wings on my chest. I stood there for a few moments, and then I broke ranks and stepped up in front of the greatest man I ever knew. The old dragoon stood there looking deep into my eyes as I saluted him, and he saluted back.

What a sight he was, all dressed in his red British uniform. Queen Victoria, the Monarch he had served, and the English people would have been proud if they could have seen him. The old man was eighty years old, but that uniform still fit him like it did sixty years before, when he had ridden the horse he had named Magic across the plains of Natal, South Africa. I learned later he had the old uniform dyed red again to bring the color out, so it was as red as it was when he wore it in his youth.

He put his hand out, palm up. My commanding officer placed my silver wings in Grandfather's white-gloved hand. Then Grandpa gently pinned them on my chest. I noticed tears in his eyes, and tears silently fell from mine. Grandpa put his arms around me and held for a moment. Then he stepped back from me and saluted me and then my commanding officer. After one last look at me, he turned and walked towards the stands where Dad and my uncles stood. The bagpipes picked up his cadence, and the notes from the song "Danny Boy" rolled over the parade field. At that moment I again promised myself that our name would always be safe with me.

After the ceremony was over and we all got our jump wings, and all the bigwigs had left. I found Grandpa and my uncles sitting in the stands. When my uncles and I had all hugged, Grandpa put his arm around me and said, "Let's take a little walk."

He told me that Dad had already left. He had signed on as chief engineer of a ship up in New Jersey, and they were going to Southeast Asia.

Grandpa went on, "I tried to get him to stay a minute or two, but he said the time just wasn't right. He's never forgiven himself for the way he just slipped out of your life."

I replied, "It's OK. Grandpa, I was able to see him in the stands. I remember he used to stand up behind the fence of the football stadium where he thought I couldn't see him. I would make a good play and look up and he would be standing there with his arms raised to the stars and then after the game, he would be gone. I know he loves me, but we still have a lifetime together. Right now I just want to be with you."

As we walked Grandpa talked. "Johnny, I know from your Book of Mormon that you believe in angels, is that right?"

I replied, "Angels are the spirits of just men, who have lived, died, and been sent back to earth to protect us, Grandpa."

Then he said, "Psalm 91:11 says. *For he shall give his angels charge over thee, to keep thee in all thy ways.* This path you have taken can be a very dangerous one, Johnny. If you are ever in peril, listen for a small, still voice. I believe with all my heart, it will be your guardian angel. Do what he tells you to do, son."

I stopped walking and turned to Grandpa and asked if he was all right.

He answered, "I'm eighty years old, son. Does that tell you anything? But Johnny, more than a dozen times, I've heard my guardian angel warn me. I did what he told me. That's why I'm eighty years old. When I go through the veil, I will petition the Lord to have the honor to be your guardian angel."

"I'll listen for your voice, Grandpa, and if there is any justice in this universe, you'll be my guardian angel. But don't leave me yet, Grandpa," I whispered.

"I'll always be with you, son, the Lord will never separate us. I bear you my testimony of that."

"Grandpa, why don't you join the church?"

"It would kill your Grandmother. Just do our work in the temple after we are gone, and I know she will accept it on the other side with me," he said with a big Irish smile.

I stood there looking into his eyes and said, "I'm not ready for you to leave me yet, Grandpa."

Then he flashed that Irish smile again and said, "Only the Lord knows the time, son. Just remember, I love you. Now get on with your life, Johnny, my boy, and squeeze as much out of it as you can. Remember, Johnny, I'll meet you at the veil, but wait one year after your grandmother dies too. I can hardly wait to lean across the altar and touch her lips."

ALMA

I remember the first time I heard his name. It was at the U.S. Army Special Forces Medical School at Fort Sam Houston, Texas. I was sitting at a table in the mess hall with a bunch of men who had no idea I was a Green Beret and that I had just flown in to attend medical school. I was dressed in medical corps whites, and my beret was sitting in my lap.

One of the men told the others at the table that there was a blue-gummer Green Beret who had just arrived to attend the next Green Beret medical school session. He told them that he had seen his nametag and his name was Blue. All the men at the table turned their heads towards the door as he walked into the mess hall, and then I realized the problem.

He was tall and proud, proud to be a black man, and I could tell he was proud to wear the Green Beret. I could see the pride by the way he wore his beret tilted down over his left eye and the spit shine on his boots. Rednecks hate black men like Blue.

The men at the table took odds on how long Blue would last at medical school. All of them were instructors at the Brooks Army Medical Training center. I was so glad that none of them were Green Berets. They decided he wouldn't last a month.

I almost wanted to get in on the bet because I knew better. I could see it in his eyes; it was the same thing I saw in the mirror every morning when I looked into my own eyes. I couldn't fail, and neither could he, because it might be the last time we ever had to prove our worth.

I stood up to leave and proudly placed my beret on my head. When I looked at them, all the rednecks' eyes were glued to their trays. I picked up my tray and boldly told them that I would tell Blue that they were concerned about him. I looked over at Blue, and he smiled at me like he knew what had just happened.

I started sitting next to him in class from the first day in school. I wanted to search his soul to find out what made him so much want to be a Green Beret, to serve a country that still had black and white restrooms and water fountains that we couldn't drink from—a country that had betrayed him and all his people so many times in the past and present.

We became good friends in the weeks that passed at Fort Sam, but we couldn't go off base and have supper together without starting a fight. If we went to a white restaurant a cop or sheriff would show up and make Blue leave; if we went to a black restaurant the same cop or sheriff would make me leave. The Jim Crow laws made it a crime, but we did it anyway and it caused us a lot of grief. I mean it was hard for a white boy from Port Orchard, Washington, to believe I couldn't go to the bathroom in the same bathroom that my black friend went in. We would take the bus to town, and Blue would have to sit in the back and I would have to sit in the front.

I learned that he was born in the Deep South but had grown up in the ghetto of South Chicago. He had quit school when he was seventeen and joined the army. Once he was in the service he finished high school and attended junior college for almost two years. He was always studying. When I and our other friends were out chasing the girls, he would be in the day room hitting the books. Besides, he would proudly tell all of us, he was married.

I believe I only saw Blue waste time once or twice in all the years I knew him. He seemed driven by some inner strength that wouldn't let him rest. Even when we were out running at night he had to beat me; we would both run until we could hardly walk back to our barracks.

I asked him once why he studied so much. He replied, "Once I learned that knowledge wasn't a big mystery, I can't seem to get enough of it, besides I think it's the only thing that will ever set me free."

Forty percent of our class failed Green Beret medical school. Blue and I were not among those who only dreamed of wearing the Green Beret but never did. We wore it.

Blue, another friend named Tommy, and I became as close as brothers in the months that passed. After medical school at Fort Sam we were sent to an army hospital in the Deep South for ten more weeks of on-the-job clinical training.

I was with Blue when he was refused service in a restaurant and called boy. When I saw the hurt and sorrow in his eyes I came unglued. I hit the restaurant owner in the face; then with two blows I dropped his fat cook. Someone jumped me from behind and pinned my arms to my sides. We struggled as he dragged me to the street. I finally broke loose and turned to face him. The best friend I ever had stood before me. Blue told me that those kinds of people weren't worth going to jail over. He asked me, for his sake, "Next time, Johnny, just walk away."

Blue, Tommy, and I went all the way through training together: the Mormon, the Boy, and the rebel—a phrase we heard whispered many times behind our backs.

The thing about it was the way Blue taught us to handle it. It made Tommy and me better men.

After all of our jungle warfare schooling was finished, Blue and I left Fort Bragg and went to Vietnam to the Fifth Special Forces. We were assigned to two different A Teams in a Green Beret compound set up in the central highlands not far from the Ho Chi Minh trail.

One night as we lay on top of our bunker and looked up at the stars twinkling above us, Blue made me promise that if anything happened to him I would make sure they buried him on the Mississippi Delta where he was born, and I promised.

I said, "My aunt Sadie wants to bury me in Preston, Idaho, next to my grandfathers if anything happens to me," but I told him not to let them do it. Then I told him about the little cemetery on Mountain View Road in Silverdale, Washington, and that if I went first that was where I wanted to sleep the long sleep until the resurrection. I told him that no matter how many medals they pinned to my chest, I didn't want to be buried at Arlington National Cemetery; I wanted to be home where I could rest under the shadows of the Olympic Mountains.

As time passed, Blue and I treated the sick and wounded and delivered the Montagnards' babies. We heard their first cries, held them to our faces, and smelled their baby breath, and we both wondered how such a miracle could happen in such a war-torn land. We treated the children for things their Montagnard parents thought were just a part of life and death. All during this time a bond grew in our hearts that I'll never be able to put into words.

We stood shoulder to shoulder and fought for our lives and mourned when a friend would die, when all our training and prayers couldn't help. All of these things are a big part of what makes up my eternal soul, son.

After six months we returned to the world, and when I reminded Blue that we had cheated the Grim Reaper, he said, "It isn't over yet."

We had been back from Nam about four months, and after more medical and jungle warfare training we were reassigned to another A Team of Green Berets and told we would be deployed back to Nam in about six weeks. So we took thirty days' leave to spend with our families.

Blue and I had gone on leave not knowing where Tommy would go next since he was assigned to another A Team. When we got back from leave we found Tommy had taken leave himself and wasn't due to return before we were to leave, which meant that we wouldn't see him again until we all ended up back at Fort Bragg.

Tommy's home was in Rome, Georgia, which was just a few hundred miles from Fort Bragg. Blue and I were sitting in the day room watching TV when I got the idea to slip over to Rome and surprise Tommy before we left. Blue responded, "That will be a good surprise, Rome is the hotbed of the KKK. We'll all three get lynched by good old boys."

Blue didn't want anything to do with driving all the way across North Carolina into Georgia with a white guy. But with his fingers crossed he gave in. Our plan was to drive straight across North Carolina and avoid South Carolina, then drop down into the top part of Georgia and into Rome. I thought it would be a piece of cake; Blue wasn't so sure.

We arrived in Rome about two a.m. and decided to get a motel room on the edge of town. That way we could get some sleep and slip up on Tommy about noon. So we picked a motel that had windows in the back that Blue could climb in and out of. Then I dropped him off a block or so away.

I drove into the front entrance of the motel and went in and rented a room. Then I parked my car in front of the unit that I had rented. As I opened the trunk of my car I looked up and down the street to make sure that all was clear. I took one of my bags into the unit and opened the window in the bathroom. I then went back to my car and had one more look around; it looked all clear. Blue and I knew the chances we were taking but thought that being in the army would give us some protection.

I turned and went into the room, and Blue was lying on the bed. He said, "I get the bed, smart guy. We may be sleeping with the fish in some swamp tomorrow, so I want to be comfy tonight."

The next morning Blue slipped out the back window as I checked out of the motel. I then picked him up at the service station two blocks down the road. We were about five miles out of town and getting close to Tommy's home when a Ford van pulled up beside us. It had a mean-looking Rome, Georgia, cracker hanging out the window holding a pistol aimed right at my face.

He said, "Pull over, blue-gummer lover, and I'll let you live."

When I hesitated, he cocked the hammer of the gun and I pulled over. I threw my Ford into reverse to try to get out of there but parked right up close to my back bumper was a big black Buick. We were stuck, and before we could run, the cracker in the window was right up beside my car with that pistol aimed right in my face.

The top was down on my convertible so I got up on the back of my seat and waited as those good old boys with baseball bats walked up to the side of my car.

Blue got up beside me and said, "Hi, guys, where's the ball game?"

Then the littlest redneck I ever saw swung his bat at me. I turned to avoid the blow, and he hit me right between the shoulder blades. Boy that little turkey could hit. His bat must have been a thirty-two-ounce hardball bat. The blow drove me down onto the car's steering wheel. I could hardly move as they pulled me out of my car and onto the road.

I must have blacked out for a couple of seconds and they forgot me as I lay there in the middle of the road. I came to and saw that the one with the pistol was pointing it at Blue's face and telling him he was going to die. Then someone hit me on the back again, and I slipped back into blackness.

And then I heard my Grandfather's voice say, "Laddie, defend yourself."

When I came to I could see they had tied a rope around Blue's neck and to the bumper of the van. Those crackers were going to drag him up and down that lonely Georgia road by his neck. They were all bent over my struggling friend trying to tie his hands behind his back.

Thinking I was out cold they were acting like I wasn't there. I reached down and slipped my switchblade stiletto out of my jump boot and stuck it into the leg nearest me. The tough guy with the gun screamed and fell to the road. The runt with the bat swung at my head. I ducked and held my knife up towards the sky. As the bat swung over my head, my knife ripped a huge slice in his forearm. When I had stuck the big guy he had dropped his gun almost in my lap. I scooped it up and pointed it at the six other crackers and said, "Release my friend or you will all die."

No one moved so I cocked the hammer of the pistol back into the firing position. Then I gave them one more warning, "I'm real serious, I'm a Green Beret, not just some leg soldier right out of basic training, and I'm real good at what I do. I'm going to start shooting if my friend is not standing in three seconds." They let Blue up really fast.

I bent over the big fellow and said, "Get up, porky."

He stumbled to his feet holding his leg and whining. Then I told all of them to strip and looked around for the runt and Blue. My friend was working really hard to stop the bleeding in the little jerk's arm.

I told Blue, "Just let the little weasel bleed, he was going to stretch your neck a minute ago."

But Blue just ignored me and finished wrapping the runt's arm. After everyone had stripped I told them to head for the woods, and then I slashed the tires on the van and the old Buick with my boot knife.

They all took off for the cover of the woods and I kicked their clothes into the creek running beside the road. They all ran but the two guys I had cut; they just stood there looking at me like they didn't understand.

Then Blue said, "Can't you see, Johnny, they are going into shock."

The little guy had a cut that went from his wrist to his elbow. Blue had used the first aid kit I kept in my car to treat the little guy's wound. The little nerd was holding ice that Blue had taken from our ice chest on the wound. The big jerk was holding the sides of his leg with both of his bare hands as blood flowed down to his ankle. All of a sudden I wasn't mad at him anymore, and the medic in me took over.

I told him to lie across the hood of my car. I then took the first aid kit from Blue and went to work on the big redneck's leg. As I worked on him it sank in how badly I had cut him. I tried to stop the bleeding with pressure but it just wouldn't stop. So I opened the wound with my finger to try to see what was making it bleed so badly. My boot knife had an eight-inch blade on it, and it had gone all the way through the leg. I couldn't see why it was bleeding so badly from the entry wound, so I opened the exit wound up further with my knife and found the problem. I had cut the femoral artery. I pinched the artery together with my fingers and told Blue what I had found and that the guy would bleed to death if I didn't tie off the artery.

I told Blue to get the fishing box I kept in the trunk of my car. Blue read my mind. As he opened the box he took out some nylon fishing leader and quickly tied a knot around both ends of the artery. It was like we were in combat again. I then made a big butterfly suture out of tape and pulled the cut closed really tight. Then I wrapped a big dressing over the wound and almost as an afterthought I wrapped the big guy's belt around his leg and tied it really tight.

Then I turned to Blue and said, "These guys have lost a lot of blood. We have to get them to a hospital in Rome before they go into deep shock."

We stood there looking at each other; we both knew what that meant, but there was no other way. We would just have to tell our story and take our chances with good old southern justice; maybe the army could act fast enough and get us out of this mess.

Blue said, "Put your clothes back on. We're taking you into Rome to the hospital."

They got into the back seat of my car, and as I pulled out around the van I threw their pistol into the creek. We had gone about a mile when the big guy reached over and put his hand on Blue's shoulder and said he was sorry and swore that he would never be so stupid again.

Then the runt put his hand on my shoulder and said, "We were drunk, it was all so stupid; I promise we will never tell anyone you cut us with that knife, and I'm sorry I hit you with my bat."

When we pulled into Rome the big fellow told Blue to lie down on the seat and not to get back up. We got to the hospital, and I took them inside. They both shook my hand and said, "Good luck."

As I started up my Ford I told Blue, "We are getting soft as grapes. Those two good old boys are going to rat on us."

I looked down at Blue and could see the imprint of the rope they had tied around his neck. I put my hand on my friend's shoulder and said, "Alma, mi cordzon, I got us into this mess I'm going to get us out of it." And we slowly rolled out of Rome.

We found the main road and decided we could see Tommy when we got back to Fort Bragg. The sooner we got out of there the better. We hadn't gone ten miles when a sheriff's cruiser pulled up behind us. He tailgated us another mile before he finally pulled us over.

The big old redneck cop walked up beside us and leaned on my car door; he was probably one of the grand Dragons of the KKK. The first thing he did was ask me why Blue was lying on the seat; I told him he was drunk. He asked for my license and Blue's I.D., then he walked back to his car and got on the radio. When he finished checking us out he came back to the car and handed me my license and Blue's I.D.

Then the big old boy leaned over in my face and said, "I have two men laying in the emergency room all cut up and you two sitting here with blood all over you and the hood of your car. Now I want to know what happened?"

Then he looked over at Blue and said, "How about you, boy, do you a have a good reason for having blood all over you?"

My friend looked right in his eyes and said, "We were drinking beer with a friend when he broke a bottle and cut himself while he was cleaning it up. We had a real hard time stopping the bleeding."

By then I realized that the two guys in the hospital had stuck to their promise and not told what had happened. I then butted in and told him that that was all there was to it. I then wrote down my name and rank and told him that we were attached to the Special Forces training group at Fort Bragg and if he needed us he could reach us there. I told him, "We are headed for the border and we will not stop until we are in North Carolina."

He stood there with his hand on his pistol, staring at me, and said, "Don't ever come back to Georgia again."

Blue knew I was going to say something dumb so he put his hand on my arm to try to stop me. But it was too late; I had gotten mad when he called Blue 'boy,' and I didn't like the way he was standing there with his hand on his pistol.

I said, "I will go anywhere in this country I want."

He slowly let his hand slip down from his gun and waved us on. I pulled back onto the blacktop and headed northeast.

"Why can't you just learn to keep your big mouth shut?" Blue ask.

Then he slipped down on the hot leather seat and said, "We have to get back to Vietnam where it's safer."

I looked in the rear view mirror, and the sheriff was following close behind us. He followed us all the way to the county line, where a state trooper sat on the side of the road. The sheriff pulled off to the side of the road, and the state trooper took his place about four car lengths behind us. The trooper followed us all the way to the North Carolina state line and stopped.

It started to rain so I pulled over and put the top up on my convertible. With the top and the windows rolled up we could talk. I told my friend that I was sure President Kennedy was going to change things down here in the South.

Blue thought about that for a while and then said, "That's the big difference between the whites and the blacks: the whites wonder what the president's going to do, and the black man just wonders what the sheriff's going to do."

We were beat up more than I thought and ended up staying in Womack Army Hospital for two days. You could see the rope marks around Blue's neck, and I had two bruises that looked like a bat all the way across my back. It was so painful I had to lie on my stomach. While we were in the hospital two FBI agents came in to talk to us. But we wouldn't tell them anything. They left with a warning that if we got into any more trouble we could lose our secret clearances. Blue and I knew that if that happened they would throw us out of the Green Berets.

I said to Blue, "Look at the bright side of it, if they did that maybe the rangers at Fort Lewis would pick us up. I promise you, Blue, that if you ever get to the Evergreen State and the land of Big Foot you will never go back to Dixie and good old southern justice again."

My bishop came in right after the feds left, and Blue just lay there and listened to what was said. I told him I had nothing to confess and that I was living the standards of the church and the army. After he left Blue said that he had read the book of Mormon and that he believed it, but that he couldn't join the church until he could hold the priesthood. Then he made me promise that if he died before that happened I would do his work in the temple. And I said I would.

Then he said to me, "Back in Rome you put your hand on my shoulder and called me Alma and said, *Mi corazon*, why did you do that?"

And I answered, "The name Alma has its roots in Latin, and in Spanish it means soul, *mi corazon* means my heart." He had forgotten that Spanish was my second language.

Then Blue said, "Johnny I have read all of your writings, and you sign them John Aquilla Kershaw, and I know that is not your middle name. Why do you do that?"

And I answered, "That's my pen name; if I ever publish that's the name I'll use."

Blue asked, "Where did you get the name Aquilla?"

I told him that was my uncle's first name. I said that my grandfather Kershaw had spent two years in Greece, that he had studied Greek mythology, and that Aquilla in Greek myth means the Eagle.

Then about one o'clock in the morning Tommy slipped into our room and woke us up. With that big old goofy smile on his face he told us he had heard we had visited Rome. It was the talk of the town, but the two guys in the hospital wouldn't crack.

He said, "I talked to one of the guys you stripped and ran into the woods and I knew it was you two." So we told him

55

our sad story and that we just wanted to see him before we deployed back to Vietnam.

He leaned back in his chair, looked up at the ceiling and said, "The South just isn't ready for you two yet, one of these days you just won't come back and then what will I do for fun?"

Then I said, "Hey, you guys, you know that statue of the rebel soldier in town, well let's slip down there one of these nights and paint the face black and put big red lips on it."

"Johnny, you know that little redneck may have had the right idea when he hit you with that bat," Blue responded with a laugh.

Within three weeks we were back in Vietnam assigned to the same area we were the first time over. It was kind of sad because some of the Montagnards we had been close to had been killed or taken captive by the Viet Cong. It was very hard to lose a Montagnard friend. They were almost like little children the way they looked up to us. It was like losing one of our own; their whole families took us into their inner circle, and we became a part of their tribe.

Then one clear, crisp morning when the sky was so blue and the world so quiet, Blue stepped out of our bunker and into eternity. A sniper's shot split the day and my life wide open forever. Blue fell back down the steps of the bunker and into my arms. I felt the warm, sticky blood seeping into his thick black hair. I cried his name and pleaded for him not to die. He opened his eyes and looked up at me, but I know he didn't see me. I don't know why but I flashed back to the time he told me that he was doing all this for his wife and baby, so they could hold their heads high and never be ashamed of their birth.

They found us seconds later as I set there soaked in my

black brother's blood. All I could say was, "I won't leave him until he is in the ground of the Mississippi Delta."

I refused to let them put him in a body bag. They couldn't make me let him go. Someone packed my duffle bag for me, and my commanding officer cut special orders for me to be Blue's honor guard and travel with him back to the world. I wrapped him in a blanket and then carried him in my arms as we flew in a chopper to an army morgue on the coast of Vietnam. I waited while they prepared Blue for the long, sad journey home and left him only long enough to wash his blood from my body and get dressed in my class A uniform, the uniform of an honor guard.

I flew all the way with my back against Blue's flag-draped coffin and thought of all his dreams, of his wife and baby boy, and then I cried again.

The door of the big starlifter was opened at Travis Air Force Base in California. I couldn't believe I was back in the world again. It seemed a million miles from Vietnam. They told us we would have a layover until the next day. I was told to go to the transit barracks and wait for morning.

I said, "No, I'm staying with my friend."

"You can't stay with him, Sarge, he'll be in the morgue," the flight nurse told me.

"Fine, that's good enough for me too," I responded.

The pilot of the starlifter put his hand on my shoulder and asked me if I wanted to see a doctor to get something to help me sleep.

I said, "No, nothing can help me sleep right now."

They got me a cot and blankets, and Blue and I spent another night together. The most beautiful Air Force flight nurse I had ever seen came in three or four times during the night to check on me.

The next day we flew on towards Mississippi and landed at an air strip two or three hours later. From there they put us on a train for the last part of our trip to the Mississippi Delta. Again they tried to separate us, and again I refused.

They thought they had a crazy Green Beret on their hands, and maybe I was—crazy with sorrow. But that was fine; at least they stayed away from me. I sat on the floor of the baggage car with my back against Alma's coffin. I remember so well the sound of the train whistle and the wheels churning under us. Oh! What a lonely feeling. And I wondered if that lonely feeling was the same feeling my father felt as he rode the rails during the Great Depression.

After what seemed like years had passed I heard the whistle blow long and sad. The train slowed to a stop, then the door of the train opened and before me stood Blue's family and friends. They rushed to me and pulled me to my feet and held me in their arms, and we cried together. Blue was home and so was I.

Again I refused to be separated from him and stayed the night in the waiting room of the funeral home. The thing I remember most about that long night was the black and white cruiser driving around the block every half hour just to keep an eye on me. It would stop, and the cop inside would flash his spotlight through the front window right in my face. It was still 1964, and I was still a white man in a black man's funeral home in Mississippi.

We laid Blue in the ground when the morning was young, the sky was clear and blue, and the air was crisp, just like the morning he died. I wasn't surprised when I was told that there were black and white cemeteries in the South. I was dressed in my class A uniform with Blue's beret on my head; his wife insisted that I take it. I asked the family if we could open the casket one more time; they approved, and I placed my beret on Blue's chest. I took my place at the head of the coffin as they closed it for the last time.

The army honor guard fired twenty-one shots into the sky and then the lone bugler standing on the hill behind us blew the heart-rending notes of "Taps" over that hallowed ground. I was amazed that all the soldiers from Fort Rucker were black. I saluted as they folded the flag from Blue's coffin, three cornered. Then they presented it to me, and I turned and told the family that it was gift from a grateful nation. I kneeled down beside Blue's widow and laid it in her lap. Then she took me in her arms, and we cried again.

Then with permission from Blue's mother I stepped back to the head of the coffin and, with the power of the holy priesthood I held, dedicated the ground where Blue would rest until the resurrection.

Some called him "boy"; I called him "Alma." Man plans, and God laughs.

BLACKJACK CREEK

When I left the Mississippi Delta after we buried Blue and I said my last goodbyes to his family and friends, I flew back to California with two or three things in mind. First to get my car from Uncle Virgil and to get home to Washington State. Second I wanted to see Mount Rainier and smell the water of the inland sea Puget Sound. And last but not least I wanted to swim in the swift, cool waters of the snakeless Blackjack Creek.

Being an army combat medic made it feel like Vietnam was never far behind me. I was due to return in less than three weeks. I felt more like a witness than I did a medic. I was the last person some of my buddies ever saw. I was the last witness to the deep love they had for the loved ones they were about to leave behind. I witnessed their tears and the dreams they had, the dreams they took with them into eternity. I was an observer of the strength of mortal man as they fought to live one more second. Their faces were the things I wanted to leave behind me as I pushed my Cobra Mustang up Interstate 5 going home. The most important thing of all, I was a witness of the truth of man's immortal soul. I saw the peace in my friends' eyes as they were about to pass through the veil to a better place. It all seemed to have put a heavy burden on my shoulders, and at times I would have gladly traded places with them, because it seemed to have made me the keeper of their dreams.

But at that time on that California freeway I just wanted to see and feel the coolness of Blackjack Creek as it surrounded my tired body. Just maybe the waters could quench the fire in my soul. But most of all I longed to sit with my family for a little while. To listen to their questions about the war and pretend I knew the answers. Hopefully just by being with them again I could go back to a simpler time and get some kind of feeling back in my soul. Maybe my bishop would let me pass the sacrament with the deacons like I did when I was a twelve-year-old boy, or maybe the cool waters of Blackjack Creek could make me feel closer to Heavenly Father like the day I was baptized. It seemed Blackjack Creek had almost taken on mythical status in my mind as my soul was slowly dying in Vietnam.

Mom had told me they were going to have a family reunion the day I got home and not to take my time about getting there. But first I had to feel the water of Blackjack Creek and slip back into my youth once again. Then after I felt reborn I would sneak up to the back door of the house, kiss Mom and feel her arms around me. I then would hold my little brother in my arms, kiss my sisters, and hope to feel my soul start to come back together again.

Then I awoke out of my daydream to the flashing of red lights and the front of a black and white squad car in my rearview mirror. I must have been speeding while I was dreaming of home. What was I going to tell this trooper? That I wasn't thinking straight, that my soul was in pieces? Should

I tell him about Blue—would he even care? No, I would try not to say anything, not let him see any weakness. Besides he had more than likely seen more in a week on this highway then I saw in six months in Vietnam.

I stepped out of my Mustang and walked around to the rear and waited while he checked my license plate number to see if my wheels were hot. As I stood there looking towards the mountains in the east I could feel his eyes watching me. Maybe he was trying to figure out what he had.

The trooper got out of his car and as he walked up to me he checked me out really closely. His eyes moved from my jump boots to my beret and then to the ribbons on my chest then back to my dead eyes.

He said, "May I see your driver's license, and do you know how fast you were going?"

"No sir, I was dreaming of home. It seems like I've been gone a thousand years or more."

It had just come out before I knew I was talking. I lowered my eyes so he couldn't see the moisture building up in them. He stood there looking at my license and then his eyes turned towards the mountains that I had been looking at moments earlier. He handed me my license and said, "Here, Sarge, it's a warning this time, but slow this Cobra down. I want you to get home too."

As I pulled back onto I-5 I looked into my rear view mirror and could see the trooper was looking out over the desert towards the Sierra Madres. I wondered what he was thinking about—maybe a brother in Vietnam. It seemed the Dragon was touching us all. Everyone seemed to be looking for answers to this thing called war. The whole nation seemed to be searching its soul.

I didn't stop driving until I got to Grants Pass, Oregon,

where I found an old, run-down motel and settled down for the night. I lay awake in my bed thinking of Blue and Vietnam for most of the night. I didn't dare sleep because I knew the Dragon was just waiting for me to close my eyes and then we would fight through the dark time until the dawn. I lay there longing for my family's arms around me and the water of Blackjack Creek to cool the fire I felt in my soul and wondered if I would ever get over Blue.

Then I awoke with a start; I couldn't believe I had fallen asleep. But most of all I couldn't believe the Dragon had not invaded my dream time. It had been a long time since I had rested in peace. I lay there in my bed listening to the sounds around me and the cars hurl past out on I-5. I felt rested for the first time in a long time maybe old motels do that to people. It seemed the closer I got to home the better I felt.

I slipped out of Grants Pass and onto I-5, pointed my Cobra north and put my foot in the carburetor. When I got to Portland I turned onto I-80 and retraced the footsteps of my youth, east to Troutdale. I wanted to see the old dairy farm I lived on when I was a little boy; the place my brother and I almost burned to the ground while playing with matches.

There was an old side road that took me past the dairy farm down to the Columbia River where I parked my Mustang. The sun was high in the shy and hot so I stripped down to my shorts and dove into the cold, clear water of the Columbia where I had played as a little boy. There were no snakes or traps and the Dragon only lingered in my dream time. I looked to the sky and said, "This is what it's all about, isn't it Lord? This must be the way you meant this life to be. Please help me forget Blue, Father, please give me back my happiness."

I stood there near the edge of the river and let the sun dry my skin. Northeast of me stood a mountain that I thought must be Mount Adams. Looking at those beautiful white peaks I suddenly realized why my Indian ancestors believed that the gods lived on the mountaintops. I dressed and drove back up to I-80. I again turned my Cobra east. I wanted to see Bridal Veil Falls and touch the rock wall that bordered the highway. This is where my father and uncles had met during the Great Depression. They had belonged to President Roosevelt's Conservation Corps and had built the walls with their bare hands. It always amazed me that a bunch of kids could have built something like those walls. They stretched all the way through the Columbia Gorge and beyond over the Blue Mountains to Grandfather's house in La Grande, Oregon. As I parked my Cobra and reached out and touched those rock walls my father and uncles had labored on, I knew I would never pass and take them for granted again. I would never drive by them again without an afterthought.

I was home, but was it for the last time? No one can understand what that word 'home' really means until their soul almost dies. "Home," my father's favorite song from *Phantom of the Opera*, was that because Dad's soul had almost died in the Pacific so many years before.

Mom was waiting for me and she would worry if I were late. So I turned my Cobra around and headed west back to Portland. I took a right onto I-5 and headed north again. Off to my left just before the bridge that crossed the Columbia River and into Washington was Jantzen Beach. The roller coaster that Dad took me on when I was about seven was still there. It was a ride of my life. I would rather ride a flaming chopper into the jungles of Vietnam then get back on that thing again. The only fact that made it a fond memory was that I was with Dad.

The bridge over the Columbia River was a blur as my

Cobra ate up the miles as I headed north towards Blackjack Creek and home. When I passed Vancouver I saw off to my right the old veterans' hospital. I couldn't help wondering if someday that was where I would be. Maybe on this next trip to Vietnam I would lose control of my mind as the Dragon and I fought for our lives. Maybe one night in my dream time we would fight one too many times and reality would slip away. My uncle Larry told me one time that most of the veterans' hospitals were mental institutions. I guess that shows you what war can do to the minds of man.

The traffic on I-5 came to a standstill. I couldn't see if it was an accident or highway construction. The reason I couldn't see ahead was because I was looking at the back end of a huge semi-truck. It kind of reminded me of the life of a combat medic; we were always looking at the same thing. The view never changed, it was always the backside of some grunt. If we weren't looking at it on patrol, we were trying to sew it back on after it got shot off.

As the traffic started to move I was able to see what had happened. Lying beside the highway was a dead cow, and a hundred feet further was a huge piece of scrap iron—all that was left of a little British sports car. It looked like it had hit a brick wall instead of a cow. The state troopers were pulling a blue tarp over the whole car. That's when it dawned on me that the dead driver was still trapped inside that tangled piece of iron. I felt the strings of my heart being pulled as I realized someone's family would cry tonight. Maybe the shield was starting to come down; maybe with Alma's death it was coming down.

After I had traveled another hundred yards I came upon a pickup truck lying on its side with the door of the cage that he was carrying his cow in lying wide open. The farmer was sitting on the ground holding his head, sobbing over the fact that he had caused the death of a man. A state trooper was trying to console him, but the tears wouldn't stop. I pulled over and went to the trooper and told him I was a medic— could I help? The trooper looked at me with sad eyes and said, "Only if you can bring back the dead, Doc."

I got back in my Cobra and headed north. The rest of the trip seems a blur until I topped the crest of the Tacoma Narrows Bridge. I could see the old restaurant on the left as I passed it. The taste of ice-cold Orange Crush pop and the feel of the icy cold brown bottle all came back to me. This was the place where my brother and I would refresh ourselves after the long climb up from the bottom of the bridge. But there was that smell, the smell of the inland sea, Puget Sound.

Then as I was going up the hill from the bridge toward Gig Harbor I could see where one of the old houses we had lived in had been torn down to widen the highway. But in my mind I could still see the old house and the chicken coop where my brother and I had raised rabbits. Things change. Then I prayed that they hadn't changed Blackjack Creek.

At Bethel Road and Highway 16, I downshifted my Cobra into third gear and almost sucked the doors off of a state trooper's car. When he saw me it was too late. I had caught him completely off guard, and before he could get his car back out onto the highway and after me, my Cobra was a mile ahead of him.

I crossed Blackjack Creek where it runs under Highway 16. Then I threw my Cobra back into fourth gear and shot up over the hill at Sidney Road. A half mile from Tremont I downshifted to third gear again and hit the brakes, turned right, and shot up the hill to Pottery Hill Road and went left. I knew that if I were to lose the trooper, it would be right there. But of course I never saw his lights go on I was so far ahead of him; maybe he never came after me. When I turned onto Pottery Hill Road I slowed down to twenty-five miles per hour and coasted down the hill to Bay Street and Sinclair Inlet, Port Orchard, Washington (Home, the world).

The sun was just going down behind the Olympic Mountains to the west, and I could smell and see the inland sea. I was back home with my family and the Blackjack Creek of my youth. These were the only things that kept me going when all seemed lost, when it seemed the Dragon was about to win, when I was about to lose my very soul.

It was 7 p.m., and I didn't want to go to Mom's home just yet. I wanted to buy some blue jeans and a couple of sweatshirts; I didn't want my mother to see me in uniform. I had taken special pains to keep her from knowing that I was a Green Beret; she would have never stopped worrying if she knew. So I had decided that after my swim in Blackjack Creek I would change out of my uniform before I went home. It was funny: I wanted my aunt Sadie to see me in my uniform but not Mom. Aunt Sadie would worry, but not the same way Mom would. Besides, I wanted to watch the sunset and look at the lights of Bremerton coming on first.

I started my Cobra and drove down Bay Street through Port Orchard to Blackjack Creek. It was getting to be too late to make my way down Blackjack Canyon to the old swimming hole, so I decided to do it in the morning. But just knowing it was there and unchanged had a calming effect on me, and I had this overwhelming desire to sleep—something that I hadn't had since I first set foot in Vietnam.

I left Blackjack Creek behind me and drove another mile to Retsil and parked in the foot ferry parking lot. Then I walked out onto the ferry dock where my brother and I had fished for so many years. I could see schools of perch swimming around the old dock's pilings. At the very bottom I could see large starfish as they slowly made their way across the sand. They moved so slowly I couldn't see them move; all I could see was a little track they left behind them. Parts of the old dock were rotting away. I could see that it wouldn't be long before they would have to stop foot ferry service to this side of Port Orchard or build a new ferry dock.

I went back to my car and just sat there. It seemed Blue was so far away, but always on my mind. I knew I would never wipe his memory from my mind. I guess that's the chance you take when you love someone. I would have to learn to live with it or die a bitter old man. How could I sit there and feel so safe when my brothers were still in harm's way? But knowing that I would be back with them soon was a good feeling—a feeling only a man with a dozen brothers could ever feel.

But as I sat there watching the harbor lights slowly come on I'd never felt so safe. It must have come from being at home. Then somewhere in the dark time there by the inland sea I fell asleep. I hadn't known such sound sleep in years.

When I awoke I could feel a shadow cast over me. I looked up through the window of my Mustang, and above me stood an old man all bent over and leaning on a cane. I rolled the window of my car down and said, "Hi."

The old man looked me over really closely with his sparkling steel blue eyes and said, "Soldier boy, I see."

"Yes sir, I am."

The old man stood up as straight as he could, wrinkled his eyes, and replied, "I was in the army way back in 1917. I fought the Germans in France. How about you, son, you see much action?"

"A little, sir, but not as much as you, I'm sure."

He looked into my eyes and said, "Of course you have, I can see it in your eyes; you are hurting. I promise you, son, that when you are my age it won't hurt as bad and the memories will fade. The thing you will remember the most will be the brothers you served with, that will never go away."

The old man turned and walked up the hill towards the old veterans' home. I had forgotten about the old soldiers' home. Maybe that's where I would spend my last days, like this tough old soldier.

I decided I wanted to go swimming in Blackjack Creek before I went to Mom's home. So I found a place to buy breakfast and then drove up the hill to the old high school and walked out onto the football field. I could almost see the lights and all the people in the stands. What good days those were just playing ball. I spent the rest of the morning just walking around Port Orchard. At noon I went to a clothing store that I remembered from when I was a youth and bought some jeans and sweatshirts. I would change in my Cobra after I went swimming.

Then when the sun was high in the sky and it was hot I had lunch, after which I drove my car in behind the A&W Root Beer stand and parked. I knew from years of coming here that I was just above the old swimming hole. I got out of my car and looked at the back door of the root beer stand, and looking at me was a big, raw-boned man. He recognized me and waved, and I waved back and turned to go down into Blackjack Canyon.

I could hear the rushing water from the creek below, and I knew the swimming hole was straight down the hill as the forest seemed to close in around me. The trail that led down into the forested canyon was well used. Other boys had found our swimming hole.

When I was at the bottom of the canyon and standing on the high bank of the creek, I stopped and looked around me. I could feel someone watching me. I could feel their eyes on me, but they weren't the eyes of the Dragon. I felt no threat, so I stripped down to my shorts.

I stood there on the clay bank that formed the pool in the creek. When I had located the huge rock that lay just below the surface of the water I plunged to the right of the rock into the deep, cool, clear water of Blackjack Creek. I had dreamed of that moment as I lay along the Ho Chi Minh trail in Vietnam, waiting for the Dragon. The memories of that creek were the only thing that saved my soul from the madness of that jungle.

The current of the creek pushed me around the curve of the deep pool the rushing water had formed many years before and into the shallower waters of the creek. I stood up, and there on the bank sat the eyes that I had felt. Two teenage boys sat in the only spot where the sun could get through the thick canopy of the forest. This was the same place my brother and I had sat to dry our bodies so long ago.

The oldest boy smiled up at me and said, "You have made that dive before."

I replied, "My brother and I have spent the best part of our lives right here."

Then I told them to move over and share the sun. The cold water had chilled my body. They ask me what kind of soldier wore a green beret. I tried to explain and then told them I would much rather swim then talk about the army. I climbed back up on the steep bank of the creek and plunged in again. I twisted my body and slipped past the huge boulder and let the current sweep me through the bend in the creek that formed the deepest part of the pool.

The two boys and I swam until the sun no longer made its way down through the little hole in the forest canopy. They reminded me so much of my brother and me. Both boys stood there asking me questions as I dressed. I told them that I was going back to Fort Bragg the next week, leave my car, and then go back to Vietnam.

The oldest boy said, "I think I would like to be a paratrooper someday."

I bent over and folded my pant legs down over the tops of my jump boots, and as this boy spoke of being a paratrooper I could almost see him in the jungles of Vietnam.

I stood up straight, looked him in the eyes, and said, "Then enjoy this place because someday its memory may be the only thing that gives you the will to go on, when dying would be easier."

I told them about my brother and that if some guy showed up one day and did a one and a half off the bank and down into the pool that would be him.

I said, "I was never able to do that, and it was a great source of pride for him."

The younger boy spoke up. "Did you have a girlfriend here in Port Orchard that was special?"

"Yes, I did. She broke up with me."

"What was her name?"

"Nancy."

"Why did she break up with you?"

Both of them stood there looking up at me. "She broke up with me because I had bad B.O., I hadn't learned about deodorant yet."

All three of us cracked up.

Then the small one asked, "Was she good looking?"

"She sure was," I replied.

"Where is she now?"

"She went to BYU looking for someone that knows about deodorant."

Then we cracked up again.

It had been a long time since I had laughed like that. Then I changed the subject and went on to explain that the war in Vietnam would be a long one and I hoped they never had to go. Then I started back up the hill to my car.

The older boy called to me. "When the salmon run in the fall I'll smoke one for you and save it till you get back next summer. We will eat it right here on the banks of Blackjack."

I turned and looked down at them and said, "I'll be back for that salmon."

I got back to my car and changed from my uniform into my new blue jeans and sweatshirt. I hung my uniform up behind me with my ribbons and jump wings facing away from the window so no one could see them. Then I rolled my beret up and put it in the big pocket of my uniform jacket. Then I hung the other sweatshirt I had bought in front of it. I didn't want Mom to know I was a paratrooper, let alone a Green Beret. As far as she knew I was just an army medic, and that was the way I wanted her to keep thinking.

After dinner that night my mom and sisters were sitting in the living room talking and my little brother Jimmy had gone to play. We had been talking for about an hour when Jimmy came into the living room from the kitchen. He had been in my car and found my uniform. He stood there with my uniform jacket all the way to the floor and my green beret down over his ears. Mom stood up and walked all the way over to him and stood there looking at my ribbons and jump wings.

She pointed at my jump wings and said, "Are you a paratrooper?"

Then she took my beret off Jimmy's head, turned back to me, and said, "Don't tell me you are a Green Beret. You have been in the army for five years—when were you going to tell me, when you are dead?"

She fell down on her knees in front of me crying, and as she clutched my beret in her hands she pleaded with me to get out of the army and please come home.

She said, "It's not bad enough that Larry is in the veterans' hospital, when will it end—when you are in a pine box like my brother? I can't believe that you lied to me."

Then I got my voice back and said, "I didn't lie to you, Mom, I just didn't tell you."

She took my face in her hands and screamed, "That's lying, Johnny. Didn't you see what war did to my brothers and your father? I knew there was something different about you. I could see it in your eyes and the way you held me; you held me like you would never hold me again."

My little brother was crying and clinging to Mom, and before I knew it my sisters were crying and holding her. I ask Mom to have a little faith in me that I was trying to make up my mind about staying in the army or getting out.

She said, "I'll make your mind up right now. I want you to come home."

I replied, "It's not that easy, Mom. I have another year to serve. I have to go back to Vietnam one more time."

She made me look her right in the eyes and asked me, "When you were missing in action you said you were hiding. Now I want the truth from you—tell me what happened."

I sat there looking at her for the longest moment, then I told her, "I can't talk about it right now. That's all I can tell you right now, Mom, without breaking down. Is that what you want from me, do you want to see me cry?"

They all held me in their arms as I fought back the tears, then I said, "My brothers and I are the best the army has; if we can't get out of this war alive than no one can. I swear I'll be fine."

I didn't tell them about Blue; if I had they would have never let me leave.

Before I knew it my time at home was over. I kissed my mom and sisters and little brother good bye and started my journey back to Fort Bragg and then on to Vietnam. This would be the hardest part of being home. I had put my visit to my brother at the veterans' hospital off until the last.

I was comforted by what I saw as I drove through the main gate of the veterans' hospital. The street leading into the grounds of the hospital were lined with huge old fir trees a hundred feet tall. A beautiful green golf course lay off to my right. The buildings were old, Spanish style, and well maintained. The lawns around all the buildings were a deep green and manicured.

I found the main building and asked the operator manning the switchboard where my brother Larry was. She asked me his last name and I told her and said that I was sorry I didn't give it to her in the beginning. I realized then how nervous I was.

Then she said, "I'm sorry, sir, your brother has requested no visitors."

I told her to please tell him it was his brother John. I could hear her talking to the nurse as the nurse passed this information on to Larry. At first he said his brother John was dead, so I showed my I.D., and finally he said he would see me.

The operator looked at me with sad eyes and said, "He is on Building 64 floor B south."

I thanked her as she gave me directions how to get there.

I parked my Cobra and walked between the buildings as I was directed. I passed a building clearly marked Building 4. Just as I passed it somewhere from above came a dreadful, mournful scream. I started to run but turned and looked up at the source of the dreadful sound. There was a huge porch that had been completely enclosed by thick wire fencing. It looked more like a cage than a porch. Perched on the hand railing and clutching the wire fencing was a man who had turned into something other than human. I turned and made my way to Building 64 as two men in white pulled the screaming veteran from the wire fence.

All around me were men who looked down at the ground; it was like they couldn't look me in the eyes. When they did look at me I didn't see any signs of life—it was like they were walking dead. Was my brother one of these men? If he was, what could have happened to change him so? Had the Dragon won?

Building 64 was the farthest ward from the main building. I took the stairs up to the main floor and asked a nurse for directions to floor B. The head nurse let me into the ward and took me to the day room. At first I didn't recognize my brother as he sat motionless among the other veterans watching TV. I walked up behind him and placed my hand on his shoulder. He turned and looked at me, stood, placed his arms around my shoulders, and said, "I thought you were dead and that they were lying to me when they said you were here." Then he placed his face on my chest and began to cry.

I turned and ask the nurse, "Can he go outside with me?"

She took me aside and said, "Yes, but you must stay with him at all times—he is on suicide watch—and be back in one hour."

We stepped out onto the front porch and walked down the steps to the ground. Then we walked down to the shore of American Lake. The two of us sat there looking out over the lake at Mount Rainier. Time seemed to stand still as we sat there in the morning sun. Then I turned to him and asked, "What is wrong, why are you in this place?"

He lowered his head and said, "I'll tell you, Johnny, but you have to promise that you will never tell anyone."

So as we sat there he told me what had happened. What he told me, he has taken to his grave and so will I, but I know Heavenly Father has forgiven him. After he told me what had happened I told him to go to his bishop and that I knew the bishop would tell him it was just something that happens in war.

Then he went on. "I can't see colors, Johnny. I know the sky is blue, but to me it looks gray. I know your beret is green but it looks black, and I know your eyes are blue but they look gray. My depression is so great they are going to start giving me shock treatments tomorrow. With that and knowing you are alive maybe then I'll feel better."

I told him that I had done things in Nam that bothered me, too. However, they would never get me in that hospital. I asked him to go home and swim in Blackjack Creek and to act like Vietnam never happened. Then I asked him if he would like a blessing, and he said he would. So there on the shores of American Lake I laid my hands on my kid brother's head and with all the power of the priesthood I held I called on Heavenly Father to watch over him in his time of need.

My brother died a young man. I believe it was from a broken heart, but how could I put that on his tomb stone?

I had just returned home from my grandfather's house in eastern Oregon when Dad came over to the Tacoma housing project to visit with us. Mom and Dad had been separated for about nine months by this time. After about ten minutes he told Mom that he wanted to talk to my brother and me alone.

We got into his car and drove out of the Salishan housing project and onto Portland Avenue. Dad turned right down the hill towards Shantytown. Then he finally broke the silence, "Did your grandfather say anything about me during the last two months you have just spent with him?"

I spoke before Larry could. "The only thing he told me was that you could have left us in a better place than this housing project."

Dad replied, "Son, there are worse places in this old world than a housing project, and I'm about to show you one of them."

I waited for Dad to say something else, but he just kept driving like we needed no further explanation. We turned off Portland Avenue onto Highway 99 and headed north towards Seattle. Dad drove a very short distance to the Puyallup River Bridge and then did something that really surprised me. He turned and drove down under the bridge and parked. He got out of the car and just stood there looking towards the hobo jungle he had told us never to go near. He waved to us to get out of the car.

The shanty town was hidden there under the railroad trestles. The little shacks were built among overgrowth from the Puyallup River. It was near the railroad tracks, which made it really easy for a hobo to step out of the brush and catch another train to nowhere. This sanctuary for broken men had been there since the

Great Depression, maybe before. I couldn't believe the direction we were headed, as my brother and I got up beside Dad.

"Why are we going to this place? Haven't you always told us never to go here?" I asked in a fearful voice.

He stopped and looked down at my brother and me with those cold, steel blue Marine Corps eyes and said, "I lived here before I knew your mother, years before you were born."

He told us that there was no work in his hometown of Preston, Idaho. So he had ridden the rails during the Great Depression and had just ended up there on the banks of the Puyallup River. Then he met Mom and his whole life changed, until the day the Japanese bombed Pearl Harbor and he lied about his past and enlisted to fight in the Second World War.

He stopped and looked around us and then said, "I must tell you the story of what happened because your grandfather has said that if I didn't he would. He feels that there is a lesson to be learned from my story. So as much as it hurts, I'm telling you now what happened to me when I was a boy not much older then you. But first I have to show you this place."

We walked into Tacoma's hobo jungle. I remember how bad it smelled, and there was trash lying among the little shacks. I got even closer to Dad and said, "I'm scared."

"You should be, son, this is a hard place, but just stay by me I still have friends here," he almost whispered.

Dad led the way and said, "I visit them every now and then, just to talk about old times on the rails. I can't believe it's 1956 and nothing has changed."

As we made our way through the little town of shanty shacks, someone yelled at us. He asked us what we were doing. Then he saw Dad and smiled as he yelled through a toothless grin, "Hey, it's Boise Jack!"

Before I knew it we were surrounded by the toughest looking old men I had ever seen in my short young life. I never knew anyone called him Boise Jack. Dad told us later that everyone in the hobo world had a nickname. Dad introduced us to a dozen old 'bos. We visited with his old friends for an hour or two, and then Dad stood to leave.

As we departed an old man stepped in front of me; his black eyes looked deep into my eyes, and he said, "Do you know who your father is? He's the 'bo that became a Marine. Has he told you of the things he saw in the Pacific, of the fights he fought? You should always respect him."

Then Dad stepped in between us and said, "No, Saul, I'll tell them when I'm ready. I'm going hunting for deer next week. If I get anything, I'll bring you guys some steaks."

As we walked out of Shantytown one of the old men said, "If you boys ever get into trouble come to the jungle and we will protect you, Boise Jack's sons."

When we were out of hearing range, Dad told us, "I never want you to return here. If you get into trouble go to the police or the church. But this is the last place I want you to go for help."

He led us down to the banks of the Puyallup River and sat down, and we settled down beside him. It seemed like an eternity before he finally spoke. "I was eighteen years old when I made a terrible mistake and stole some money from someone. I was living in real hard times. The Great Depression was upon all of us. I left my father's farm in Preston, Idaho, and went to Boise looking for work. But I couldn't find any and got mixed up with the wrong people and made some real bad choices. I was too proud to go back home and face my father broke. So out of desperation I agreed to fight in a bare-fisted fight. If I won I would get fifty dollars. If I lost I got nothing. The fight was very vicious and bloody, because both of us needed the money badly."

We just sat there looking down at the river, then Dad went on. *"When it was over I was the only one left standing, but the man who had set the fight up was gone. I went looking for him, and three days later I found him in a card room in Nampa, Idaho. When I asked him for my money all he did was laugh at me. I asked him again, and the fat man just called me a punk and told me to get lost. I hit him twice before he went down, and then I took all his money and ran. It took two weeks for the law to catch up with me... The story came out that he was a city councilman and that he set up illegal bare-knuckled fights just for fun and a little extra spending money during the hard times. But the law didn't care—I had beaten and robbed one of their own. I was the one that would pay for the fat man's broken jaw and missing money."*

I had never heard my father talk so much in all the years I had lived under his roof. Dad told us he had pleaded guilty because he was and that it had only taken that old stiff-necked Mormon judge five minutes to take two years of his life away, for taking what he felt was his.

He told us to learn from his mistake, that even if it feels right, it may be wrong. Dad hung his head, and it seemed like everything turned silent. It was like the Puyallup River quit running and the Milwaukee Road train on the trestle up above us froze in place. I had never seen my father hang his head before.

Then he spoke again. "Mother was a devout Mormon and refused to visit me in prison; she was too ashamed. She had forgiven me for shaming our family—all of her letters were full of love. But she just couldn't walk into that prison and see her son in a cage. I never saw Mom again after those iron doors closed behind my back. Mother died six months after I went to prison."

He told us that the same judge who had sent him to prison ordered the Idaho State Department of Corrections to let him go home for the funeral. They made him go in a prison car with a driver and guard. He arrived just as the graveside services were about to start.

Dad said, "I asked the guard to please remove the handcuffs, but he refused. I pleaded with him, but he still said no. So I ask him to just leave because I didn't want to stand by my mother's grave with irons on my wrists."

He told us that when his eight sisters realized what was taking place, they took things in hand. They surrounded the car and told the driver that everyone at that funeral was related or very close friends and that no one was leaving that cemetery until their brother Jack took his place beside their mother's grave. The guard turned and unlocked the handcuffs and they dropped to the metal floor of the car. Then his sisters opened the door and pulled him to his feet. By this time everyone had surrounded the car. There must have been three hundred people; the whole town was there. They walked arm in arm with him to his mother's grave.

Dad said with a small grin, "That guard found out what me and my brothers had learned years before: nobody messed with our sisters."

With Dad's father on one side of him and his sisters standing all around him, his oldest brother dedicated their mother's grave. Then his brother asked the Lord to bestow a blessing upon their family and friends. Dad said, "When the final words were spoken I raised my head to find all the family friends had slipped in between me and my family. They all hugged me and shook my hands and told me to hurry home."

We sat there watching the huge smoke stacks on the Tacoma tide flats belch smoke and waited for Dad to continue.

He almost whispered, "I never realized they cared so much and the world that seemed so cold that morning now seemed warm. It was like they never heard the chains as they fell from my wrists and hit the bare metal floor between my feet."

He stopped talking and looked up at the sky like he was trying to think of what to say next. He told us that the next year was the longest year of his life. The state released him on a hot summer day, and he made his way to the rail yard near Boise. He waited for two days for the Union Pacific's L.A. Express.

Dad said, "L.A. was real laid back in 1933, something I needed real bad. I couldn't go back home and face my family. Somewhere in the night the box car I was riding got switched, and I ended up in Salinas, California. I picked fruit and lived in a hobo shanty town; prison had made me tough so the 'bos left me alone.

"Then one cool Salinas morning I hopped a train that took me even further from my mother's grave. All the way to Dallas, Texas, and then from there to the city lights of the city so great they named it twice: New York, New York. But by then it was winter and real cold so I slipped down below the streets of the city and only came out to stand in the soup lines with other desperate men."

He went on, "I lived in the dark places and slept beside the steam pipes that laced the New York underground and kept the citizens warm in their tenements on cold New York nights. When spring came I hopped a train that took me all the way to Tacoma's shanty town."

He said it took him almost two weeks of riding the trains and that when he reached Tacoma he was so glad to put his feet on the ground again for good. He said that he lived there in the bum jungle on the banks of the Puyallup River for about six months. Then he joined President Roosevelt's Conservation Corp and built rock walls along the road that stretches along the south bank of the Colombia River. The work took him from Bridal

Falls, *through the Columbia Gorge, and all the way to the Blue
Mountains in eastern Oregon.*

He said, *"That's where I met your uncle Wesley, who took
me home with him to La Grande, Oregon, and that was were I
first set eyes on your mother. I loved her right from the start, and
in a few short months we were married in Boise. I never told
her I had been in prison. It seemed we had trouble almost from
the very beginning, I guess that's what happens when you start
a relationship with a lie. I had terrible nightmares of things I
couldn't forget. Prison took away all of my self-esteem, stripped
me of my name, and gave me a number that is still written in my
brain. I would be sleeping, and the sound of steel doors slamming
shut would sit me upright in bed. Your mother couldn't figure
out why I had such dreams. I couldn't bring myself to tell her my
dark secret, and the only thing that would silence those slamming
steel doors was whiskey. But that stuff only made me mean, and
I was always looking for a fight."*

Then Dad set us both in front of him so he could look us in
the eyes and said, *"Then after the war broke out in 1941, I lied
about my criminal record and joined the Marine Corp. I was in
boot camp when you were born, Johnny. The Marine Corp gave
me back my self-esteem, but the war has hurt my soul."*

Then somehow he blocked out everything around us, the river,
the train and cars going over the bridges above us, and said, *"I
would rather see you die on some lonely battlefield, than to have
to watch your souls rot in some dark prison. Promise me you will
never forget this story I have told you. But most of all remember
it is true and it's about your father, not some stranger or a movie
star. I made a terrible mistake and I will never stop hearing those
prison doors slamming in my dreams." As we sat there watching
the huge stacks of the pulp mills of Commencement Bay belch*

smoke into the sky above, we strained to hear his whispered words: "Remember, boys, a beggar's rags may cover as much pride as judge's robe."

SADIE

When I left my brother Larry at the veteran's hospital in Tacoma, Washington, I started my trip back to Fort Bragg. I drove on to La Grande, Oregon, and spent the night with my grandmother. I told her about Grandpa's spirit being with me whenever I was in mortal danger, and she believed me. That night I visited my grandfather's grave when the stars and moon had settled over the Grand Round Valley. I sat there with my back resting on his tombstone and dreamed about the nights we sat on his front porch and traveled to distant lands as we played chess and he told me of the things he had seen in faraway lands. But for some reason all I felt was a deep sense of loss.

The next morning I left La Grande and drove for hours along what was once the Oregon Trail. It was my intention to be in my Aunt Sadie's home by dinnertime. But the trip was longer than I remembered from the last time I was there, so I slept in my car along the Snake River near Twin Falls, Idaho.

I was so tired I slept until the hot sun awoke me at noon.

I got a hamburger in Twin Falls and then started my trip on to Preston and Aunt Sadie's home.

When Aunt Sadie opened her door all the aromas of her cooking came pouring out at me. It always reminded me of the last time when I sat at her table. You see, no matter where I had been, I made sure that my path took me back to this special lady's home. It seemed she always had the answers to things that bothered me, so it was like her home was a shelter from the storms in my life.

We ate supper, and then I helped her wash the dishes. When we were all done we sat in her living room and talked for hours. I told her all about Mom and how she was working so hard to raise my little brother and sister all alone. I told her of all their dreams and hopes.

She told me about all the things she had been doing in the church. But most of all about all my cousins who were serving missions. She told me about David O McKay and all the growth the church was going through under his direction. Aunt Sadie told me about the time he had dedicated Uncle Scofield's grave.

She said, "I stood as close to President McKay as I could, and he held my hand. He was a general authority then and one of Uncle Scofield's best friends. I could hear every word he spoke. I still remember the spirit that was there as he blessed our family."

Then somewhere in the night she asked me to account for myself. I told her what I had been doing since I had seen her two years before. Then with tears in my eyes I told her about my best friend Blue and the way he had died in my arms in the jungles of Vietnam.

When I had finished she asked me, "What else is bothering you, Johnny?"

"I have killed men, Aunt Sadie, and it is pulling my soul apart."

Then Aunt Sadie said, "You are a soldier, Johnny; soldiers kill people. You didn't kill with hatred did you? Or kill a prisoner of war?"

"No, Aunt Sadie, I didn't kill anybody that wasn't trying to kill me."

"Johnny, you have to get out of the army and come home. We are bishops, elders, quorums presidents, Relief Society presidents, and Sunday School teachers. We aren't soldiers and Green Berets. You have served for almost six years now, and I want you to come home."

I replied, "I'm trying hard to decide whether to stay in the army or get out and come home."

She answered, "We must pray about it. The Lord will give you the answer."

Then we knelt there in her living room and prayed together. She ask Heavenly Father to please teach me that no matter how many medals the army pinned on chest and no matter how many diplomas I ever earned, someday I would stand before Jesus Christ and there would be a judgment. And at that judgment Jesus Christ would brush aside all the medals and awards of this world and look at the scars on my soul. She ask Heavenly Father to teach me that Jesus would ask me about each scar and after I explained each one, he would ask me if I got back up from each terrible blow. Than she asked him to teach me how important it was to be able to say, "Yes, my Lord." Then she closed in the name of Jesus Christ.

The next morning she walked me to my car. "What kind of a car is this?" she asked.

"It's a Cobra Mustang, Aunt Sadie."

She pulled me down to her and kissed my cheek. "The

next time I see you I want you to be in a station wagon filled with little children."

"I don't know Aunt Sadie, I still have to decide."

She stood there looking up at me for what seemed to be an eternity and then she said, "I want you to stop in Layton, Utah, and visit your uncle Scofield's grave. Then I want you to call me back here and tell me what you have found. There is something there I want you to see."

I left Preston, Idaho, and drove south past Cub River and on to Logan and lower Cache Valley. When I arrived in Layton I asked directions to the cemetery. When I found it I parked my Cobra and walked to the center of the graveyard. I stood there looking at all the tombstones and felt overwhelmed. How could I find Scofield's grave? I walked around the cemetery for a good hour or two in the hot sun. All the tombstones were different sizes and different colors. Some were small, some big, but all marked the final resting place of someone's loved one. The ground between the stones was carpeted with green grass that was trimmed by the hands of someone who loved his work.

I was about to give up when I spotted an old man sitting on a marble bench in the shade of an old elm tree. I walked over and introduced myself to him. I told him I was looking for my uncle Scofield's grave and asked if he could help me find it.

He smiled at me and said, "He's buried over there," and pointed to the part of the cemetery that I hadn't looked in yet.

The old man said, "How long have you been in the army, son?"

"Five years, sir."

Then he said, "My wife is buried here. I come and talk to her most every day."

"You must have loved her dearly."

"Yes, and I still do; she is my wife forever. She was the happiest person I have ever known."

I patted him on the arm and walked to Uncle Scofield's grave. I stood there in the hot afternoon sun and read the engraving on the marble stone that marked his grave. But I couldn't see what Aunt Sadie wanted me to see. I sat down on the green grass and studied the headstone trying to feel something. Then I noticed that my aunt Rebecca was buried there too. But I knew that wasn't what Aunt Sadie was trying to get me to see. Then I noticed two smaller headstones, each marked with girls' names. They must have been two of my cousins, and they were all buried together side by side. I was sure that this was what Aunt Sadie wanted me to see.

I went back to my Mustang and drove to a phone booth in the middle of Layton and called Aunt Sadie. I told her what I had found and waited for her approval.

She said, "Is that all you saw, Johnny, four head stones?"

I quietly said, "Yes."

"I want you to go back to that cemetery and keep looking at those headstones until you see what I want you to see," she replied.

I answered, "But it will be getting dark soon, Aunt Sadie."

"Then take a flashlight with you, but don't call me back until you see what's on those headstones."

So I went back and set there looking at those marble stones. The sun was setting in the west over the Great Salt Lake Valley. And as it set it was casting shadows among the headstones, and I was getting very uneasy. I thought about just getting in my Cobra and restarting my trip to Fort Bragg. But I knew I would have to face Aunt Sadie someday, so I stayed.

Just as the sun went down completely the old man got up from his bench and walked over to me.

He said, "Are you OK, son?"

"Yes sir, I'm fine, but it looks like I may be here all night."

"What are you looking for?"

"I don't know, but my aunt Sadie says that there is something special here, but I just don't see it."

The old man took the flashlight from my hand and pointed it at my nameplate on my uniform and said, "So you are a Kershaw. What a shame the way they all died at the same time. I was a young man when it happened. I remember David O. McKay dedicated their graves. People came from all around."

I took the flashlight back and flashed its beam from stone to stone, and sure enough, they had all died on the same day. I must have been blind—why hadn't I seen that?

I asked the old man, "What happened?"

He said, "I'm not sure anymore, but it had something to do with a train."

I said, "Goodnight."

I then made my way back through the headstones to my car. This had to be what Aunt Sadie wanted me to see. I called her and told her what I had found.

She said, "That was what I wanted you to see."

She told me that Uncle Scofield and Aunt Rebecca had taken two of their teenage daughters to Lagoon to do volunteer work for the church. They had worked all day and were returning home when they attempted to cross the Southern

Pacific Railroad tracks, at which time the Southern Pacific LA Express hit them and they all died instantly.

She said, "Johnny, when that train took their lives they were doing the work of the Lord. But most importantly they were doing it as a family, and they passed through the veil together. You see, Johnny, families can be forever if we just live the way the Lord asks us to live. It didn't end there at that railroad crossing. They are a family for eternity. Now you come home, son, and start a family. I don't want you to die in some far-off jungle."

I stood there in that phone booth and looked out over the great Salt Lake Valley and realized how much my family had given to this place and how much I belonged here. All of a sudden this great feeling of peace came over me. It was the same feeling I got when I looked at the inland sea (Puget Sound). I needed to belong, and it had to be soon.

Then Aunt Sadie said, "Johnny, are you still there?"

"Yes, Aunt Sadie, I'm still here."

"Your mother and I want you to come home as soon as you can. When you were missing in action we almost died."

"I wasn't missing in action, Aunt Sadie, I was hiding."

"Don't make light of this thing, Johnny. You come home."

"I love you, Aunt Sadie. I'll call you soon, and tell you what I'm going to do."

"OK, Johnny, you drive that little white car carefully. It has too big an engine for such a little car. I love you, son, goodnight."

I left Layton and drove to Salt Lake City, where I decided to spend the night. I rented a motel room close to Temple Square and settled down for the night. Before I went to bed I took a walk to Temple Square. I stood and looked in wonder at the walls of stone my grandfathers had help build.

The gates were shut and locked, and as I stepped close I wrapped my hands around the hard, steel bars of the gate, took my beret off, bowed my head, and asked the Lord to please help me decide what I would do with the rest of my life.

When I had finished praying a voice came out of the darkness. "Son, can I help you?"

There on the sidewalk stood an old man dressed in a suit, and his hair was as white as snow. At first I thought I was seeing an angel but then he put his hand out to me and introduced himself as a missionary in Temple Square.

He said, "I'm sorry the gates are closed now, but you can come back in the morning if you wish."

I replied, "No, I think I have found the answer I've been looking for, thanks."

I left Salt Lake City the next morning and drove down through Provo. Then I headed up through Price Canyon, where I took a left at a junction in the road that took me over into Wyoming. All the time I was thinking of Aunt Sadie and the things she had told me. Then somewhere in Wyoming I happened onto a place called Little America. I stopped and got something to eat and called Aunt Sadie again.

She answered the phone. "Hello, Johnny."

"How did you know it was me?" I asked.

"The Lord always answers my prayers, Johnny."

"Then you must know what I'm going to say."

"You tell me, Johnny," she replied.

"I'm coming home, but I have to go back to Vietnam and fight the Dragon one more time. Please pray for me."

She thought about that for a moment then said, "Tell me,

Johnny, this Dragon you speak of, this Viet Cong, does he believe in God?"

"No, he is Godless."

We were silent for a long moment. Then she said, "He is the one I will pray for, because he will be cast into hell for what he is doing to the poor, innocent people of Vietnam. You just remember what it means to be a soldier of Helaman."

I stood there in that phone booth amazed at the wisdom of that lady.

Then she went on, "How can you lose, Johnny? Just guard your soul, and if you die and the veil is parted, your family will be there to greet you on the other side and your mother and I will bury you next to your grandfathers here in Cache Valley."

Aunt Sadie was a special lady. I hope we all have such a woman in our life.

Next to God we are indebted to women, first for life itself, then for making it worth having. —Bovee

NINE DRAGONS

The mad sounds of the jungle were all around us. It always seemed to me that the jungle had a life of its own. The morning sun was just starting to warm the emerald hills of the central highlands of Vietnam as we made the patrol of the outer perimeter of our compound. The morning mist hovering over the forest reminded me of the mist that covered the huge old growth of the Olympic Rain Forest back home in Washington State. Sometimes it would cause me to flash back to the times my brothers, father, and I would be stalking the rain forest for the huge Roosevelt Elk. It was like a knife was being plunged into my heart and homesickness would turn the emerald forest into a black and white photo. If I lingered in this flashback too long I would find myself sitting next to my brothers on the front row pew in our little chapel waiting to pass the sacrament on a Sunday morning. But then I had to snap out of it because lingering in the past too long while on a combat patrol could cost me my life. It seemed like having flashbacks was the only way I could keep my sanity, only it had to be at the right time.

We had gone full circle and had just joined up with the

other half of our patrol. There were seven of us (me a Green Beret) and six Montagnards (the native people of the central highlands). Three of the Yards penetrated deeper into the jungle, while the others and I stayed closer to the open ground that separated our compound from the jungle. We had just joined back up and were deciding which was the best way back through our own mine fields when, out of nowhere, the *Dragon* appeared.

The Viet Cong patrol seemed to materialize right out of the ground. They had us dead to rights, with no way out. They bound our hands, then hammered our backs with the butts of their AK-47s as they drove us towards the west, away from our compound. An hour into our trip one of the Viet Cong hit the Montagnard in front of me in the back with a violent blow with his rifle butt. The Yard tripped and fell to his knees, and as he started to get back up the *Dragon* drove the bayonet attached to his rifle through the Yard's neck. I was dumbfounded. The message was clear: none of us would walk out of this jungle alive.

They pushed us hard, and I lost all track of time. Then we stopped just a few miles from the Mekong River and Cambodia. No food or water was offered—why feed dead men?—and we never asked for anything. Instead, they wrapped my arms around a thick stake at the elbows and then pulled my wrists and forearms until the tree limb was pressed in firmly to my spine. Then they grossed the rope in front of me and pulled my right wrist over to my left wrist and tied them together. When they finished with that they tied a rope around my waist and tied that rope to the rope attached to my wrists. I could hardly breathe, and my hands were already turning purple.

As the *Dragon* patrol tied the Yards the same way, I was

hog-tied. The one Viet Cong that seemed to be in charge drove the butt of his rifle into my stomach. The third time he hit me I threw up. I had never felt pain like that in my life. He hit me a dozen times before I passed out and was relieved of my pain.

I entered a misty land, and the eyes of my mind could see as far back as 1946—all the way to when I was a five-year-old boy. The thing I could see clearest was my brother and me standing on the cliff in front of our house watching for Dad's ship to come home from the war. Our home overlooked Rolling Bay on the east side of Bainbridge Island, Washington. Mom had told us that Dad would come home soon; he would come from the north down through the San Juan de Fuca Straits on a big, gray ship. She told us that he would be with other soldiers coming home from the war in the Pacific. She also said that if the fog wasn't too bad on the day it came we would be able to see it. On a good day we could see all the way to Everett; beyond stood the white peaks of Mount Baker. Once we saw an eagle as it swooped down to the beach below us. We would take old bread from the house and lay it on the edge of the cliff, and the sea gulls would land and fight over it. Now and then a crow would dart in and steal a piece of bread from the bigger birds. As we stood there waiting for Dad's ship to appear I remembered back to a day when Mom was sleeping and my brother and I got cold, so instead of waking Mom up we decided to build a fire in the fireplace.

It looked so easy when Mom did it, but no matter what we did we couldn't get the fire to start. Then I remembered how my uncle had started a fire with gasoline, and I knew my mom had an extra bit of gas in a can out in the garage. So I went and got it and brought it into the house. The paper we had used to start the fire was still smoldering so I opened the can and threw it on the paper. The whole can erupted in my face. The flames burnt the sleeve of my shirt off, my arm, and the whole right side of my body. I had never felt so much pain in my life. Mom's car had broken down, and she didn't have the money to fix it. She ran to the next-door neighbors and asked them to please help her take me to the doctor's office. I can still remember the pain as the doctor broke the blisters on my arm, face, and chest. Then he put some kind of ointment all over the burns and wrapped my wounds in gauze; that hurt worse than the first burn. It hurt for days, and Mom would sit up at night with me as I cried and cried. I remember thinking that if Dad were there he could stop the pain. He was a marine, and everyone knew they could do anything.

When I woke up the *Viet Cong* were cutting all of our clothes from our bodies. The leader of the Viet Cong patrol was telling the Montagnards that before they died he would show them that Green Berets weren't gods. Then he threw a nylon rope over a limb high up in the closest tree to me. I thought they were going to lynch me. I waited for the rope to be wrapped around my neck. Instead they tied it to the wooden stake that they had woven between my elbows. Then four of the Viet Cong pulled on the rope until my feet were about six feet off of the jungle floor. All in turn, my five Yards were hung the same way.

At first I could hold myself up, but within a half hour the weight of my body started to pull me down and forward until my chin rested on my chest. I looked over at the Yard scouts and could see they were starting to slip forwards too. But I could see no pain in their faces. Within an hour the pain was so excruciating that it felt like my arms were being ripped from my shoulder sockets. Still I could see no pain in my Yard friends' faces.

Man! It took everything I had to hold back the tears. I

wasn't trying to show anyone I was a god, but I was surely going to show them I was a man. I wasn't a god; I would tell them right out if that was what they wanted. But I knew there was more to it than that. The leader of the *Dragons* was mean, and I knew there was a reason to his madness. All I had to do was wait and I was sure he would fill me in on what he wanted.

I tried to think of home, of Blackjack Creek and Minter Creek, Port Orchard and football games on Friday night, and what Vaughn Bay was like at this time of the year. These were places I went to as a boy when my world seemed turned upside down. I wondered if they even existed. Then the morning came, and the rope lowered me to the ground until the tips of my toes just barely touched the jungle floor. The leader of the *Dragons* stood there before me with a pair of vise grips in his hands. He didn't say a word, just put the vise grips on my left testicle and tightened them until the testicle popped. I closed my eyes and held back my breath, screams, and tears. Then he took his K-bar knife from its scabbard and held the sharp edge of the blade to my chest. At first I thought he was going to castrate me but instead he cut a ten-inch laceration from my armpit to the nipple of my chest. And then he cut the other side of my chest the same way. I refused to scream, but I passed out again.

I was back in that misty world looking down at those scars from the fire on my right arm and wondering if Dad would feel sorry for me or would he be mad at me for doing such a dumb thing. My brother and I sat there on that cliff in front of our little house and watched for weeks that turned into months. Two little boys looking for the father who went away when one was just a baby and the other was still in his mother's belly. Mom explained that the ship was slow because it had to stop at different islands to pick up other soldiers. She explained that they were bringing the ones that had been there the longest home first and that Dad was there longer than most of the others. We played there on the cliff and watched for Dad's gray ship.

We played war with wooden rifles that Grandpa had made for us. We would take turns being the Japanese. We built forts and even dug a cave in the side of the cliff, and all the time we watched for Dad's ship. We would watch until the lights of Seattle across the bay would light up the night sky. Then early one morning Mom came from the house with tears in her eyes and told us that the radio had just said that Dad's ship had just past Fort Warden. There was an early morning fog, and we strained our eyes trying to be the first one to see it. The smoke from the ship's stack was the first thing we saw. Then like a ghost, it slipped from the mist of the inland sea. Dad was home— this man I hadn't seen since I was two years old. I tried to remember but I couldn't.

I slowly awoke, and the hours seemed like an eternity as I hung there. I closed my eyes and tried to visualize what it was going to be like to die. Then I remembered the first time I saw a live dog with its front legs tied behind it in one of the open-air markets of Saigon. I bought it and freed it down near the edge of the jungle. But I knew he didn't have much of a future. Is that what I looked like, that poor dog hanging there in that meat market on Tu Do Street in old Saigon? I prayed to the Lord that if I was going to die, please give me the strength I needed to die without betraying myself. I had seen the aftermath of the mutilations of some of my buddies, and I knew they had lived long enough to witness that mutilation. I needed the promise of the Holy Ghost to get through this. Somewhere under the cover of darkness I slipped into a semi-conscious state. When morning came there was a beam of light coming down through the canopy of the jungle. I thought I saw an eagle swoop down right at my face; it was so real I flinched. Was this what the plains Indians saw as they did their sun dance? Was this a sign from my Indian grandmother Rising Star? Was she telling me I could die like a man? When the light slowly came back and the sun began to heat the jungle, I was dropped from the tree limb to the ground. With my hands tied and my feet bound the landing I made was not a pretty sight. They pulled me to my knees, and the *Dragon* that was in charge spoke to me in perfect English. He told me that he had gone to the United States and attended U.C.L.A. and that he had come home to nothing but poverty. The only way he could see to get out of it was to rid his country of first the French and now the Americans. The *Dragon* questioned me for hours. Over and over again he asked me the names of the men on my "A" team and the source of our intelligence in the area. All I would do was answer him in the Montagnards' dialect. He would get so mad the blood vessels in his forehead would pop out. He told me to answer him in English or he would blow my brains all over the jungle floor. So in the best English I could come up with I told him, "So pull the trigger, you little dink."

He held the muzzle of his rifle to my forehead, and I could feel his hands shaking, he was so mad. Then the promise of the Holy Ghost came over me as I waited to go beyond the veil. There was no fear. I knew my grandfather was just a split second away. Then the *Dragon* pulled back and hit me in the neck with the butt of his rifle and said, "I see your game, you American pig; you will not die that easy."

At first it all seemed like a game, but somewhere it went beyond just giving them information. It seemed like I would have been giving them my soul if I told them anything. I blacked out, and they brought me back with the ammonia capsules they had found in my rucksack. They made me kneel on the jungle floor. Then they lowered one of my Yard scouts from above, dragged him over to me, and made him kneel in front of me face to face. I looked deep into my friend's eyes as he knelt down, and in his Montagnard dialect he told me not to tell them anything. The *Dragon* put the muzzle of his 9mm p-38 pistol to the temple of the Yard scout's head. Then he asked me, "What is the source of your intelligence in this area?" Once again in my best Montagnard dialect I gave him my name, rank and serial number.

The Viet Cong pulled the trigger of his pistol, and my friend's head seemed to explode. They forced me to look at the body of this defiant, brave little Montagnard as they disemboweled him. They held me so tightly that I couldn't look away. They did it just to show me what they were going to do to me if I didn't talk—only when they disemboweled me, I would be alive. I couldn't comprehend the reality of what had just taken place.

The blows to my head and the shock of what I had just witnessed put me back into that foggy, distant dreamland as they left me to lie there on the jungle floor. My mother held me in her arms as tears ran down her face. We waited for what seemed like hours. In the meantime Larry and I made telescopes out of newspapers and watched as tugs nosed Dad's ship into Pier 91. Mom called all of her family on the island and told them Dad was home. Hours later, the phone rang. It was Dad telling Mom what Blackball ferry he would be coming over to the island on. We were all there to meet him when the ferry slipped through the waters of Eagle Harbor and nosed up to the dock. All of Mom's family stood there waiting with their own thoughts of what Dad would be like.

He was a legend. He didn't even have to go to war. He was 4-F but he lied about his criminal record and joined the Marine Corps. My grandfather would count the invasions he was in on; he numbered them on the door of his pickup— twenty-one in all. I remember people asking Grandpa where he was now, and Pop would tell them that he didn't know, that all his news was a month old. Grandpa painted six purple hearts below the numbers. I remember asking what they were, and he told me that the Japanese had shot him six times. Grandpa knelt beside my bed that night and as I said my prayers, I started to cry and ask Heavenly Father to tell the Japanese to stop shooting my daddy. The next day Grandpa painted over those purple hearts and never talked to me about them again.

I worried that Daddy would think I was ugly because of the scars on my face and arm. I was two years old when Dad went to war, and I wondered if he would still love me or if the scars would make him turn away. They were slowly fading, and the doctor had told Mom that maybe I wouldn't scar too badly.

As the last car on the ferry cleared the car deck, the first thing I saw was his white hat. His uniform was blue and hard to see in the car deck tunnel. But that hat got whiter and whiter as Daddy got closer to the sun. Then the sunlight sparkled as it rested on his medals. He stopped to let his eyes adjust to the sunlight. The bill on his hat and his shoes shined like patent leather.

Then I looked at his face, and he looked tired and older than I imagined he would be. As Dad came towards us, Mom's whole family ran to meet him. Everyone but my brother and I. He just said a few words, then walked by all of them. He stopped for a moment and looked down at us. At first I thought I could see his chin start to quiver, then nothing. He just got in the old car and sat there looking straight ahead— the marine who couldn't cry.

My mother stood there covering her mouth like she was trying to hold back tears. Then she kissed Grandpa goodbye and took us by the hands and put us in the car. He hadn't even kissed Mom. Was he acting like this because of me? Was I that ugly?

The rope yanked me from that dreamland and back up into the tree and reality. The pain was something that only another person who's been hung like that can ever know. When the reality of what had just happened sank in I asked the Lord to take me home with him. I looked up and could still barely see the other four Montagnards hanging there, just waiting their turn. The *Dragon* knew he would never break the Yards. They hated the *Dragon* worse than death itself. Not only that, the Yards weren't privy to the information I had. If I broke it would mean the end to a lot of good people who were on our side. That was why he was working on me. He knew I wasn't afraid of dying but he was betting I was scared of the way I died; I believed he was wrong.

Then I slipped back into that misty, distant dreamland. I was standing on the front porch of our little house at Rolling Bay, looking at my father as he sat in an old wooden lawn chair near the cliff looking north over Rolling Bay. It was like he was looking for another ship to slip silently from the mist of the inland sea of Puget Sound. Dad sat there for weeks until he finally gave up and went back to the job he had on the Blackball ferry before he went to war. I wondered if that ship would ever come in for Dad.

I came to in the middle of the night and strained to look up for the hole in the jungle canopy where the sun had shone in my face for an instant. I saw one star, and as I looked at it I ask the Lord to remember the promise of the Holy Ghost.

Then I slipped back to that distant land. This time I was sitting on Grandpa's front porch playing chess and listening to his stories of the world that he had seen. I asked Grandpa how long my dad was going to be so lonely. He thought about that for a moment and then said, "Yes, that's a good way to say it. You see, son, when you go to war and your life depends on other men, they become your family; that's all you have, your brothers. On one island that your father invaded, four thousand marines died, and he lost a lot of brothers. Yes, son, he may be lonely a long, long time."

As my dream ended I remember the old Irishman saying, "Defend your king, Johnny my boy."

When the sun came up I was barely able to see the *Dragon* standing below me through my swollen and blackened eyes that he had beaten the day before. He was standing there looking at something in his hands and then he would look up at me for a couple of minutes then look back at his hands. As hard as I tried I couldn't make out what he was holding.

Then the *Dragon* dropped me to the ground. The meanest Viet Cong I had ever seen held my miniature sized, brown Book of Mormon and Bible up to my face. I carried them in my jungle fatigue breast pocket all the time. He asked me what they were, but again; only in Spanish I stated my name, rank, and serial number. My eyes focused on my scriptures as he hit me in the neck with his fist.

Then the one member of the Viet Cong patrol that had never said anything spoke in perfect English. "When I went to school in France I met some Mormon missionaries, are you a Mormon missionary working for the Green Beret and the C.I.A.?"

I still refused to speak, and the *Dragon* hit me in the same spot on my neck, but by then the pain no longer seemed as bad. Two of the Viet Cong forced me to my knees. Then the English-speaking Dragon said, "Sergeant, we are told the C.I.A. is getting information from Mormon missionaries in other countries where my communist brothers are fighting wars of liberation. Tell me, are they doing that here in Vietnam now? Are you a Mormon missionary?"

I struggled to look up at him, and this time in German I told him my name, rank and serial number again. A blow from a rifle butt hit me between the shoulder blades, but I was able to stay on my knees. This educated Dragon had my attention, and I wasn't going down until I made it clear I was not a Mormon missionary.

I twisted so I could see his face and said, "I'm a Mormon, but I'm not a Mormon missionary, and no Mormon missionary ever worked for anyone other than the Lord Jesus Christ, anywhere in this world."

Then the beatings started all over again. The blows from the previous day had taken their toll on my body, and it didn't take long for me to black out this time. But the *Dragon* awoke me with the ammonia capsules taken from my own rucksack. They didn't beat me this time. Instead the educated one forced another Montagnard scout to kneel down in front of me. I looked into his eyes trying to find some kind of emotion, but saw none.

"Please don't do this!" I said.

Then I heard a voice I had heard many times in my life. My guardian angel, my Irish grandfather said, "Don't give up, laddie, I'm with you." I looked around to try to see him, but he was nowhere in sight. Why couldn't I see him? The shepherds saw the angels in the fields where they slept when told of the birth of the baby Jesus; Joseph Smith saw two angels; why not me?

I looked into the Montagnard's eyes, and he said, "Lamanite, tell them nothing."

Then the *Dragon* pulled the trigger of his p-38 pistol. This went on until I watched as the last Montagnard was dragged into the jungle to lie and rot, or maybe the tigers would consume them. I knew I had little time left on this earth.

On what was to be the last day of kneeling at the *Dragons'* feet, the educated Viet Cong placed a large piece of cardboard on the jungle floor where I knelt. He had written a confession he wanted me to sign. It said I was a Mormon missionary caught working for the Green Beret and C.I.A

He said. "I'm going to take your picture holding this signed confession. Then I'm going to execute you for your crimes against the people of Vietnam."

He went on to tell me that if I signed the confession I would die quickly like the Montagnards had. But if I refused, I would die very, very slowly. I had seen the results of the slow deaths these men could perform. I knew I would be alive to watch my own mutilation.

I thought of my cousin serving his mission in Bolivia where the madman Che Guevara was trying to spread Castro's revolution. Should the communists convince the poor people of Bolivia, Paraguay, or any other third world country that I was a Mormon missionary working for the C.I.A, my defenseless brothers and all their work would be in danger. I cursed myself for not leaving my scriptures in my footlocker. If there were any chance that my confession would be used to harm one of my brothers, it would be without my signature.

Two of the *Dragons* were pushing me down over the confession. Another one was holding my freed wrist and hand trying to make me sign it. I bit my tongue as hard as I could. When the blood filled my mouth, I spat it all over their phony confession.

The French-educated *Dragon* raged and struck me across my eyes with the barrel of his pistol, then he beat me back into that foggy dreamland.

I was sitting on Grandpa's front porch with Irish war drums playing on his little record player beside his chair. He taught me how Aristotle trained Alexander the Great to defeat a million— man army with only twenty five thousand men and I dreamed of being a warrior. As I started to come out of it I heard grandpa say, "Defend your King Laddie my boy."

They tied my hands again and lifted me back into the tree so my feet just barely left the ground. Before they pulled me the rest of the way up into the tree and with blood dripping down my face the *Dragon* held his pistol against my lip and said, "You will die a thousand times in the morning. But before you leave this earth you will be photographed with this confession in your hands, signature or no signature."

I hung there in that tree and strained to look up at the stars through that little hole in the jungle canopy and prayed to the Lord. I asked him to take me home with him now, that I knew it was within his power. I pleaded with him not to let me live through the night. Then something stirred way down deep in my soul as I realized that I wasn't praying to the Lord, I was whining. I was crying to the same almighty God that had stood and shook in some far away galaxy to hide his tears as his only begotten Son suffered a terrible death. I closed my prayer by asking the Lord to please have my family waiting for me as I passed through the veil. As I strained to see the stars through my swollen eyes I drifted into blackness.

I floated through the misty land of my past homes. I could feel the cool, clear water of Blackjack Creek in Port Orchard. Then I found myself back on Grandpa's front porch playing chess with that old English northern dragoon and defending my king against that old chess master. With his black chessboard set between us, Grandpa smiled at me over the black and white checked field of battle where kings and knights ruled and said,

"One Montagnard lives, Johnny my boy; now prepare to defend your king."

I had watched all the Montagnards die. What did Grandpa mean? Had the Lord taken me like I had asked or was I still hanging in that tree? Then the rope I hung by moved ever so slightly, like someone was undoing it down below. I strained to see below me through my bruised and swollen eyelids, but it was too dark. I knew it must be time to die. The pain shot through my shoulders with a new intensity as I was swiftly lowered to the ground.

The *Dragon* would drag me to the nearby village where the execution would take place. I had asked the Lord to give me the strength not to sign that false confession. With new determination I swore my signature would not be on it. When I reached the ground, two strong arms wrapped around me. Instead of dropping me to the ground, I was gently laid down. Then one of my Montagnard scouts was kneeling over me. I could barely make him out in the darkness. Then I remembered what my grandfather had said in that misty land, "One Montagnard lives."

I couldn't believe it. I had seen the *Dragon* shoot him in the head. While he cut the ropes that bound me to the limb I strained in the dark to see the wound in the side of his temple. When my arms were free I placed my hands on my scout's head to feel for the wounds I was sure would be there. But all I could find was the entrance wound—no exit wound. The bullet had not gone all the way through his head. Then I found a large knot at the back of his head. I was sure that was the bullet, but how it had traveled around to the back of his head I don't know. He must have turned ever so slightly when the *Dragon* pulled the trigger. I would look at it later but now we must run.

The Montagnard had killed all three Viet Cong who had been left behind to guard me while the educated one and the officer went to the village to arrange my execution in the morning. As I sat there on the ground trying to get my bearings and deciding what to do, my grandfather spoke to me again. "Johnny, go north to the Se San River, then follow it to the Mekong River. Then swim, son, with all your strength to the nine *Dragons*."

I took a K-bar knife and an AK-47 from one of the dead *Dragons*. Then I told the Montagnard scout what my grandfather had said. He never questioned me, just turned north toward the Se San River. When we reached the river we plunged into its cool water. The water soothed my swollen eyes and helped the sore muscles in my beaten body. We had been given no water all the time we were held by the *Dragon*. Now the river seemed like heaven, but we knew we had very little time to flee the remaining Viet Cong patrol. They would expect us to go east, back the way we had come, but we needed the river to help us since we were so weak and unable to run. The river was deep enough to swim, but both of us were so tired after a mile I decided to make some kind of floating device to help us.

I took a limb from a tree that had been knocked down by lightning and made a float for my Montagnard scout and me. The limb still had branches and leaves attached to it. This made it so we could hold on, lay beside it in the water, and be hidden from anyone on the bank of the river. We were also able to hide our AK-47s and supplies in among the limbs and leaves of our little splintered log float. I had decided to fight to the death if the *Dragon* caught up to us.

It took us three days to traverse the Se San River and finally merge with the larger Mekong River. The Mekong's water was warmer and the current slower. There were more people on the Mekong and more danger of being spotted by a Viet Cong water patrol.

My eyes had taken a real good beating and had become infected after we escaped from the *Dragon*. I felt movement on my chest where the *Dragon* had cut me three or four days before. I looked down, and the wounds from the K-bar were infected with maggots; my first thought was to crush them and wash them away, but they were cleaning away the dead flesh and saving me from gangrene, so I left them. My eyes had become so bad I couldn't see more than two or three feet in front of me. I couldn't tell if a boat was just a Vietnamese fisherman or the *Dragon*. So I stayed hidden in the leaves of the limb. We drifted at the will of the big river's current toward what I thought was freedom and safety.

There were a lot of water vipers and lizards and all the fish a blind man could catch. I thanked the Lord for his bounty, and we ate snakes, fish, and lizards till our hunger was gone. It was a real trick for a half-blind man to catch a viper. I couldn't see them until they were two feet from my face. Then I had to strike before the snake did. I didn't have time to be scared—it would all happen so fast.

Then one morning when I was pulling our little log raft to shore where we could hide for the day, I heard footsteps. I concealed myself in a bush growing along the riverbank. A Viet Cong walked right past me and reached out to grab our float and pull it to shore. My Yard friend and our AK-47s were still hiding among the branches of the log. I had to do something because I knew he would discover my friend the moment he pulled on the log. I jumped out from under the bush and wrapped my arm around the *Dragon's* neck and drove my K-bar up under his rib cage and into his kidney. It took all the strength I had left in my tired body to hold him in my arms as he died. I then pushed his body out into the river's current and asked the Lord to accept his soul through the veil, then decided to stay afloat that day.

I hadn't prayed any meaningful prayers to the Lord since the last night in the tree. I was ashamed after all the whining I had done. But I knew I had to talk to him again. I needed help and I needed it badly. It had been dark for an hour or two when I lowered my head and asked the Lord to help me. I asked for the strength to get me and my Yard friend to safety and to please tell me where the *nine Dragons* were, then I drifted off to sleep.

I found myself back on Grandpa's front porch. We played chess through the night. Grandpa was the barbarian who defended Gaul, and I was Caesar. When the chess game was over Grandpa said, "Soon you will be with your brother. But you must hide among the river grass in the daytime, then let the currents of the river carry you at night. You must do this because you are nearing the nine Dragons, and the Viet Cong patrols will increase there. Now, son, fight. Defend your King."

We drifted for two more days, hiding in the grass of the riverbank and floating at night. My Yard friend stopped eating altogether. He seemed tired of eating nothing but raw lizards and fish. But there was nothing I could do. I wasn't able to light a fire out of fear of attracting the Viet Cong. The snakes I had been catching seemed to vanish, so I just concentrated on fish.

We had to rest. We had been in the river for almost two weeks. So I took my Montagnard friend and our little log raft as far back from the river as I could and made a bed out of wreaths in a huge bush. While my friend dried out in the sun I went back to the river and threw my fish trap out into the water. In an hour I had a good carp fish. I used the driest twigs I could find so there would be very little smoke, and I started a fire. I had found a large soup can floating in the river so I cooked the fish, and then for two days I force-fed my Yard friend. I was sure the bullet had cracked his skull; he would drift in and out of consciousness. The bones and flesh of the fish made a bland broth but it brought strength back to both of us as we rested for three days. My eyes started to clear up and my eyelids parted a little at a time. On the third day, my friend seemed a lot better. I decided to cut the bullet from the back of his head. I made a small cut in his scalp. Then I squeezed, and the bullet popped out into my hand. The bullet was flat on one side and round on the other side. It had gone into his scalp at an angle and hit the skull and then followed the contour of it and stopped just under the scalp at the back of his head. I couldn't explain what had happened. That was up to the Lord.

I tied our AK-47s back among the limbs of our log float. When the sun went down I pushed off from the banks of the mighty Mekong River. This night we drifted past a big city that I thought was Phnom Penh. I never even thought to stop. For some reason my mind was set on the Mekong Delta. It must have rained back in the mountains behind us because the current of the river seemed to come alive. I knew if I could just keep going there was a Green Beret "A" detachment at Don Phuc, and maybe we could find them before the *Dragon* could find us. We had been on the Cambodia side of the River for a week, and I didn't want to take the chance of falling into communist hands now. I knew the Mekong would take us to Vietnam and safety. I fell asleep during the night and seemed to drift in and out of sleep for the next two days. I was just too tired and hurt to keep hiding so I prayed our little float was able to hide us from the eyes of the *Dragon*.

Then one morning the noise of very powerful engines woke me. By this time I could see well enough to count four boats surrounding us. But I couldn't tell if they were Viet Cong or ours. The power of the boats' engines could be heard even as they just sat there idling at rest. Then I realized they had to be Americans; the *Dragon* didn't have boats with motors like that. I raised my hands as high as I could, but my shoulders still hurt so bad I couldn't get them very far above the leaves of the log. Someone screamed at me through a bullhorn, telling me to raise my hands above my head. I told them I couldn't raise my arms. Then with all my strength I pushed back from the log so they could see me and yelled, "I'm a Green Beret, please help me!"

Then things got really exciting. Someone screamed over the boat's loudspeaker something about an American as one of the boats came to life and headed right at me. I would have dived under the water, but I was too tired. Then another American voice screamed over the loudspeaker, "Hold your position!"

I heard a familiar voice, "That's my friend, skipper!"

Someone jumped into the river and came up under and behind me. Strong arms wrapped around me, and I heard my friends voice whisper into my ear, "It's okay, Johnny, I've got you."

He pulled me over to the side of the riverboat, and strong arms from above pulled me onto the boat. My friend and I had broken bread together in Old Town one Sunday a long time ago. He knelt down beside me and asked what he could do.

I said, "Do you have any consecrated oil?"

"Yes, I do," He answered

"Well then, please anoint my head and give me a blessing and don't forget my Montagnard scout on the log"

My brother knelt down beside me and said, "It's too late, Johnny, your Yard has passed through the veil."

I started to cry. There was no stopping the tears as my faithful brother anointed my head with oil again and gave me another blessing. Then their corpsman gave me five milligrams of morphine, and before I knew it I was back in Port Orchard, Washington, swimming in Blackjack Creek.

I stayed in a big hospital in Saigon. My brother was able to stay with me for a week. He called Mom, and we were able to talk for a good thirty minutes. Mom was really upset about me being lost in action and said she had written Senator Scoop Jackson about me being in Vietnam so long. She said, "I almost died when that army officer walked up to my door. I slowly died for three years while your father was in the Pacific. I feel this war is going to break my heart."

I said, "Mom, I was not missing in action, I was hiding." She didn't buy it. She knew what the young officer had told her.

That night before my friend left to go back to his river patrol boat, I asked him, "Mark, do you believe in angels?"

He looked at me and said, "Yes! I'm a Mormon. The book of Mormon was given to Joseph Smith by an angel, remember?"

Then he got really still as he sat there looking into my eyes, and I said, "Grandpa has helped me get out of a number of very dangerous incidents since I have been a Green Beret. He talks to me, Mark."

"He talks to you?"

"Yes."

"Mark, he told me to go to the *Nine Dragons* and into my brothers' arms. Then he gave me directions of what to do. What are the *Nine Dragons,* and how did you get off the USS Chumung and onto a river boat so fast?"

He said, "The *Nine Dragons* are the nine rivers that are formed from the Mekong River as it flows through the Delta to the South China Sea. I put in for a transfer to the river boats six months ago so I could be near the real action."

I asked, "Do you believe me when I say my grandpa is my guardian angel?"

He sat there in deep thought, then said, "If anyone could pull that off it would be that old Irish Catholic, but don't tell anyone around here about this or they'll think you have been hit in the head one too many times."

"Don't worry, I won't," I responded. "Mark, I'm going back up to the central highlands as soon as the doctors will release me, I still have five months left on this mission, and that *red Chinese Dragon* told me something that the Yards have to know; you see he was taunting me by telling me the source of his information within our ranks. He was sure I would die with that knowledge. I know who is betraying us, and I believe it will cause the Montagnards to revolt against the South Vietnam government."

"If your grandpa speaks to you, listen," Mark said.

We just sat there in the dark for the longest time. Then I said, "Go get a chess board, and I'll give you a chance to defend your king.

"One more thing, Mark, I have taught the Montagnards out of the book of Mormon, and they call me the Lamanite because my great-great-grandfather was a Shawnee Indian chief, so if you hear over your radio that the Montagnards are revolting and they want the Lamanite, it's me they are talking about."

While Mark was gone I drifted off, but I felt movement in my room and I looked up. In front of me stood three Montagnard warriors, all dressed in loincloths and war paint. The Montagnard king spoke. "Lamanite, you are a Montagnard."

I couldn't believe what he was saying. I had just gotten six of his best warriors killed!

I sat there leaning back against my pillows and searched for something to say to the bravest men I had ever known. When my mind cleared, in the Montagnard dialect I said, "I know who is betraying us, once more unto the breach, dear friends, once more, or close the wall up with our Montagnard dead."

Then I was back in Joe Knowles stadium in Port Orchard. I had just made my seventh sack of the quarterback, and the game was over. I looked up at the top of the stadium, and there stood my grandfather and the marine who couldn't cry. I raised my hand to the stars, and they raised theirs. When the battle was over I walked out to the parking lot of South Kitsap High School, and there stood the old Irish dragoon. I asked him where Dad was, and Grandpa said, "He is catching a tramp steamer to Southeast Asia, Laddie."

I looked up at the stars then responded, "He is still looking for that ship carrying the souls of his dead brothers, isn't he?"

Grandpa put his arm around my shoulders and half whispered into my ear, "He may never find it, Laddie, until he passes through the veil. And when he does, I expect you to be there holding his hand."

"And I will be, Grandpa," I responded

"I have one more thing to say to you, Laddie, before we call it

a night. As you stood over that quarterback and raised your finger to the stars, I saw the warrior in you, son, but did you think of the man at your feet? I want to recite part of a poem I memorized once when I was a Royal Dragoon, it goes like this—

We build our future thought by thought,
For good or ill, yet know it not.
Yet, so the universe was wrought.
Thought is another name for fate;
Choose then thy destiny and wait.
For love brings love and hate brings hate."

I put my arm around his shoulder as we leaned back to see the stars and said, "I'll try to never forget my soul, Grandpa."

POINT

I could see the trail ahead, but in truth it was short and overgrown with thick green foliage; when I looked close I could see that another man had walked down it not long before. I remember asking myself, *What was this other man, was he Viet Cong, North Vietnamese, or maybe just a sniper who liked to kill? Had he set a Bouncing Betty or a claymore mine? How can I watch for trip wires and the trees above at the same time?*

The rucksack I carried on my back was rubbing up and down as I made my way through the dense green jungle. With each step I took I could feel a boil forming right in the middle of my back. The salty sweat rolled down between my shoulder blades and soaked its way into the flesh of the abscess. The sweat that wasn't absorbed by the abscess was baked by the heat and left a white film on my flesh. Before we had entered the jungle the sun had blistered my eyelids almost shut. These were all little things that filled my mind, the mind of a man walking the point.

Dad had to get up really early in the morning, like three or four every day. He would milk the cows then come back home

121

and rest until he had to go back in the evening to milk them again. It was when he came back to rest until the evening milking that he would catch my brother and me up to no good. It was funny we couldn't get used to him coming home in the middle of the day. The first warning we would have was the dust from the old brown pickup he was given by the farmer to drive. When he worked on the Blackball ferry up on Bainbridge Island we could hear the horn from the ship, and we would remember that Dad would be home soon. By the time he got from the ferry dock to our house we had turned into little angels. The change in schedule really threw us off and got us into a lot of trouble.

Sometimes my brother and I would wake up as Dad's pickup would leave the driveway of our home. He had to milk the cows so early that he would leave the house before the sun would come up. We would lie there in our beds and wait for the sound of that old truck to start up. Then we would slip out of bed, put our clothes on, wait by the window of our bedroom, and watch for the taillights of his truck to disappear down the old road that took him to the other farm. If we planned it right we could get a lot done and be back in our beds by eight o'clock when Mom would come to wake us up, and she would never know we had been gone.

One morning we waited for Dad to leave the driveway then we slipped out onto the roof of the front porch that was directly under our bedroom window. There sat our dog, Bob, waiting for us; it was like he knew the fun was starting early that day. We checked the barn out and even looked in on those nasty little mice. But we made sure not to bother them. From there we went into the main part of the barn and looked up into the rafters of the barn and checked out the old barn owl, and there he would be sitting watching us with those oversized, wide eyes. The next stop was the chicken coop to see if the weasel had stolen any of

Mom's hens. From there we decided to check things out on the other side of the farm where we had never been.

We found a creek about a mile from the house, and there were foot-long trout swimming with the lazy current right next to the bank of the creek. We didn't have fishing poles yet, and even if we made poles out of willow sticks we didn't have fish hooks. So we lay there trying to figure out how to catch those fish and have them for lunch.

As we lay there watching those fish, the sun slowly rose in the sky and warmed our backs. Old Bob lay down beside us, and we all fell asleep there in the warm sun. We didn't wake until the sun was high in the sky and very hot. The trout had moved over closer to the bank of the creek to shade themselves from the sun.

Now we had seen a movie where a Native American had caught fish with his bare hands, and we had Indian blood in us, so we were sure we could do the same. After all, our great-grandmother was a Shawnee Indian princess named Rising Star. We figured that there was just enough Shawnee Indian in us to help us catch those fish with our hands.

We quietly crawled to the edge of the creek bank and let our eyes adjust to the darkness of the water. Bob got right up next to us and lay there beside us and watched the water. An old crow landed in a tree on the other side on the creek and sat there looking at us; it looked like he was trying to figure out what we were doing. We soon forgot about the crow as, like magic, the ripples in the water turned into beautiful trout. I could feel my brother waiting for me to make a move. So I threw myself at the fish, but somehow that trout turned into a ripple again. All I pulled from the creek was water and some of its bottom. We settled back on the bank of the creek and lay in wait again.

That old crow started making a sound that sounded like he was laughing at us. Soon the reflections and the ripples turned to trout again and swam within our reach. I gave my brother the signal that it was time for him to try. So he crouched there and waited for the right moment. My brother was smaller than me, and when he lunged he fell completely into the creek and came out coughing and drenched.

We tried repeatedly and just as we were about to give up and go home my brother turned to Bob and said the magic words: "Sic-um, Bob."

The magic happened again as Bob took things into his own mouth. He dove into the creek and came back up onto the bank with a large, struggling trout. That old mutt had sat there most of the day and watched us almost drown, and then in one dive he caught the biggest trout we had seen all day.

By this time three or four more crows landed in the tree across from us, and each time Bob plunged into the creek and came up with a fish they would make a lot of noise. It was like they were cheering Bob on and at the same time trying to get us boys to throw them just one fish. But we didn't—we saved them all, and when there were no more trout left in the water we counted them. Our magic dog had caught fifteen beautiful trout.

By this time we could tell by the position of the sun that it was getting to be about time to end it, as we needed to go home before Dad came looking for us. However, we saw trouble coming right at us. We saw the dust from the old dirt road first and then Dad's old brown truck emerged from the center of the brown, man-made cloud. We had lost all track of time, and it was almost evening milking time. I could see that the sun was sitting right over the top of the Blue Mountains. The old man was so mad that I thought he was going to spank us right there on the road. Then he saw the fish, and his whole attitude changed.

Now Dad wasn't just any fly fisherman; he was a fish hunter. He asked, "Where did you catch them?"

Then he remembered that he hadn't bought us fishing poles yet, and his next question was, "How did you manage such a feat without a pole?"

We all looked at Bob at the same time. Dad said, "Did you catch these, boy?"

Bob just sat there looking at those fish like they were his, and Dad knew what had happened. All the way home we told Dad about the way old Bob had caught those fish.

When we pulled into the driveway Mom came running out of the house and gripped both of us by the front of our shirts and screamed in our face, "Where have you been? I have had thoughts of you falling into the canal and drowning, I've been sick out of my mind with worry."

Dad held that string of trout up and said, "Take it easy, Bea. The boys have just been fishing."

Mom screamed at Dad, "You would let them burn the barn down if they could catch fish doing it. You and your damn fishing will destroy this family someday, Jack!"

That was the first time I knew that Dad's fishing bothered Mom. But I was to learn that fishing and milking cows was where Dad found peace. That was where he forgot about the war in the Pacific and drowned out the sounds of crying and dying men. That was his sanctuary from his sad, mad dreams and the cruel world that threatened to destroy his soul.

We were good boys for a couple of days. Then one pleasant, sunny day the three of us lay on top of this big haystack that some field hands had just stacked for us. To our surprise a big water buffalo walked right under us. Now we knew that old, dry cow Dad had put into the pasture the week before wasn't a water buffalo, but we had really good imaginations.

When something like this happens and you just happen to have the greatest hunter in the world, "What can you do?"

How could we worry about Dad? Besides, he was at the main farm doing the morning milking. Our new prey didn't even know we were up above her on that haystack. We couldn't just look a gift horse in the mouth.

I said the magic word, and Bob jumped down to the ground right next to that cow and let out a big bark. He so startled that old Holstein cow that she kicked Bob about ten feet and took off the other way. Poor Bob was wobbling as he got to his feet, but I bellowed the magic word, "Sic-um," and Bob was off on the chase.

He ran kinda sideways at first but after a hundred feet he was looking good. Larry and I were cheering Bob on from the top of the haystack and he was closing ground. About fifty feet from the fence Bob reached out and nipped that old buffalo right on the tail. When that cow got to the fence she didn't miss a step. She jumped over it with plenty of room to spare and disappeared into two hundred acres of full-grown corn.

It was two days before that prize milk cow was found missing. So before Dad went to do his evening milking he started searching the pasture for signs of where that buffalo could have gone. Dad came back to the house an hour later telling Mom that silly cow had jumped the fence. He had found where it had gone into the large corn patch across the road. Dad told Mom he couldn't ever remember seeing a cow jump that far before. He said that he could see where she started her jump and where she had landed in the middle of the dirt road on the other side of the fence.

Dad looked right at me and said, "That cow must've been scared to death."

Now my brother and I grew up while Dad was in the Pacific, and he hadn't been back long enough for us to really know him yet—maybe we never would. Nevertheless, as I stood there listening to him talk I began to realize how smart a man he really was. I had a feeling that Bob and my brother and I might be in real trouble this time.

He told Mom that he had to go do the evening milking and that he would take care of the problem when he got back if it wasn't too dark; he was sure she wouldn't leave that cornfield until he drove her out.

What anticipation this caused my brother and I as we waited for Dad to come back home. We went up to our room, took up positions at our bedroom windows, and looked out over the dirt road and the big cornfield. Every now and then we could see the corn move, and we knew it was the cow moving through the field as she munched on corn; she probably thought she had died and gone to heaven. We talked how we could help Dad by taking old Bob and driving that cow back into the pasture. But then we would have to tell Dad how we did it and about the magic word "Sic-um." And then maybe Dad would put two and two together and figure out that it was us that had sent that terrified cow into exile into that corn patch. So we kept old Bob close to us and held our place at our bedroom window.

When Dad came home there was only an hour of light left, but he went into that cornfield as we watched from our commanding viewpoint at the top of that old house. He would find the cow and drive her towards the dirt road and the open gate of the pasture, but the cow would take one look at that gate and turn and bolt back into the heart of the cornfield. Dad couldn't see over the top of the corn so it made it really hard to find that old buffalo, but we could see every move she made.

Finally the sun set behind the Blue Mountains and dark slowly set on the cornfield. Dad gave into the darkness and exhaustion. He came across that dirt road and into the house. We sat there on the stairs leading up to our rooms and listened to what he said to Mom: "That cow is scared to death. I can't figure it out—she is one of the most gentle cows I have ever milked. But when I get her close to the gate of the pasture she goes wild. After the morning milking, I'll bring a horse over from the big farm and then I'll be able to see over the top of the corn and I'll drive her back across the road and into the pasture."

My brother and I went to bed and daydreamed of what it would be like to see Dad on a horse—maybe he would look like a real cowboy as he drove that old cow from the cornfield. Then I heard the sounds of his classics drifting up the stairs to our room; he was sitting in the living room. Sometimes I would sneak down the stairs and peek into the living room; he would be sitting there by himself as Mom had gone to bed. I didn't know if it was the music or the nightmares Dad had that would make him stay up late at night when we were all asleep in our beds. On the wall behind Dad's chair hung that Samurai sword that Dad had brought back from the war and would never talk about. Sometimes I would fall asleep there on the floor in the hallway watching my father stare into space.

I can remember wakening up in his arms as he carried me up the stairs and laid in my bed, then he would stand there for the longest time and look down at my brother and me, the marine that couldn't cry.

The next morning I heard his pickup leave the driveway. I slipped down the stairs and listened for sounds of Mom washing the morning dishes. When I was sure she was in the kitchen I slipped into Mom and Dad's bedroom and got into the closet where Dad kept his rifle. There up on the shelf above my head and lying next to two flags folded three-cornered were Dad's binoculars. I took the binoculars down, and I remember wondering why Dad never flew those flags, why they just stayed folded there where nobody could see them.

I slipped back up stairs, hid the binoculars under my bed, and then lay down to wait till the sun came up. I fell asleep again, until Mom woke me up for breakfast. All through breakfast I could hardly wait to show Larry what I had under my bed. We would be able to watch every move that cow made. And when Dad brought the horse from the big farm we would be able to watch the chase.

A twig snapped behind me, a reminder that I wasn't alone, and my mind returned to the stalking. Suddenly I came upon a wall of vines, and I didn't know whether I should just push through them or try to crawl under them. Was it a trap? I got down on my knees and slowly cut them and pushed each vine aside. It looked like the man ahead of us had lain on his belly and slipped under them. That told me he wasn't wearing a backpack.

I was sure he knew we were there; we had to get him before he gave our position away. It was like chasing a rat in a maze, and even if we found him it didn't mean we could take him without making a lot of noise. That was a big part of our mission: get in and get out without anyone knowing we were there.

I thought to myself that only an insane madman could hunt another human being, so this must have been an insane asylum. The birds above me didn't sing; they screamed like lunatics.

Just as I reached to cut through the last of the vines, a green tree viper dropped from above and just sat there looking at me. At first I was startled, but then with one swift move I caught him just behind the head, put him on the ground, and cut his head off. I flipped his head off the trail into the brush and slipped his body into my rucksack thinking that I would add him to my menu that night. He wasn't that big but at least I would have a little protein with my C-rations.

Larry and I spent the morning in anticipation of what it would be like to watch Dad drive that cow from the corn patch. We decided that the best position to watch this drama would be from the door in the top of the big barn where they loaded the hay into the loft. So we took the binoculars that I had stolen from Dad, made some peanut butter sandwiches, and constructed a nest in the hay by the door where we could safely watch every move that cow and Dad made.

We settled into our nest, and the wait for Dad and the horse began. Before we knew it we fell asleep. The noise of Dad unloading the horse from the back of a trailer woke us up. Dad looked like he knew what he was doing as he saddled that mustang. The more we watched the more excited we got. Larry leaned so far out the door that he almost fell to the ground and he gave our position away.

Dad asked us what we were doing and we told him that we wanted to watch him as he herded that old cow out of the corn. He stood there looking up at us for a few seconds then he told us to be careful as it was a long fall.

It was like a jungle in that corn patch, and he had to be able to look over the top of the corn. The only chance he had to see over the corn was from the back of that horse.

The search went on for hours. After a while a field hand took over for Dad so he could go back to milking the large herd of cows that he was responsible for. The field hand didn't have much luck, so when Dad got back he took over again.

It was frustrating; we could see the cow, but Dad still couldn't see it even from the back of the horse. I finally stood up in the second-story door of the barn and waved until Dad saw me. Then I pointed to where that cow was hiding, and Dad drove his horse in that direction. I forgot about Dad's binoculars in my hands until it was too late, but I was sure that he was too far away for him to see them.

Finally it got too dark for us to see anything, and Dad gave up the chase. I hurried down to the ground, slipped into the back door of the house and into Mom and Dad's bedroom, and replaced the binoculars by Dad's flags. I would get them again in the morning while he was back at the other farm milking the cows.

Dad was really quiet as we sat there and ate dinner. After Dad had finished eating he got up and told me he wanted to see me in the living room when I was finished eating. I thought sure he was going to thank me for giving him directions as to where the cow was today. I went into the living room, and he was sitting there in his big chair under that Samurai sword. He directed me over by his chair. All of a sudden I became very frightened.

He said, "Did you take my binoculars without asking me?"

I knew he had me, and I also knew that if I tried to lie it would be a lot worse for me. I hung my head and said, "Yes."

He set there thinking for a long time, and then he finally said, "If you ever take anything from me or anyone else again, I will spank you with my razor strap, do you understand? Now tomorrow after I get back from milking the cows I want you to get those binoculars and get back in that barn door and direct me to that cow."

All of a sudden I knew what that Japanese soldier felt like, when he surrendered his sword to this marine who couldn't cry. I didn't go downstairs that night and watch Dad as he sat in his chair and listened to his classics. I stayed all snuggled up in my bed and tried to imagine that Japanese soldier who had surrendered his sword to Dad—was he as scared as I was?

It was funny; I loved Dad, but I was frightened of him too. I wondered if he would ever put that sword up with those two flags on the shelf in his closet, or would he leave it on the wall until the day he died? I wondered what had happened to Dad; he didn't look like he had been wounded. I didn't know if his mind could be wounded, but how could he seem to hurt so bad if it hadn't? I only learned the answers to those questions later in my life.

The next morning I woke up when Dad's truck started in the driveway below. I watched him as he drove down the road towards the big farm. Then I went downstairs and into the kitchen. Mom looked surprised and said, "You're up real early this morning. Do you want something to eat?"

As I sat there waiting for my breakfast I said, "Grandma said that sometime war can wound a man's mind and soul. Is that true, Mom, and is Dad's mind wounded?"

She stood there looking at me a long time, and then she said, "That's a big question for such a little boy."

Then she turned and finished cooking my eggs. When she turned back to serve me my breakfast she said, "I'm starting to believe your Grandmother is right; after all, she has been living with a war veteran for over forty years. If anyone would know she should."

I was surprised and said, "You mean Grandpa was in a war?"

"Yes."

"Was he wounded?"

She responded, "Yes, that's why he limps."

"Do you think his mind was wounded?"

"He sits out on the porch at night for hours, and his eyes stalk the night like something is out there."

"I'm going to get Dad's binoculars from the closet. He asked me to help find that cow today."

"Yes, I know. He told me you were going to help him."

I went away wondering if he had told her the whole story.

Larry and I made our way up into the top of the barn as the sun started to light up the corn patch. I looked through the binoculars, and it didn't take long for me to find that old buffalo. She was standing as far as she could from that dirt road and pasture gate. She would rip an ear of corn off the stalk and stand there and munch away like she didn't have a care in the world. But she didn't know who was coming after her, and I did; she didn't have a chance.

Dad showed up about nine o'clock and saddled that mustang. When he walked out of the barn he looked up at me and Larry and said, "Are you ready, Johnny?"

I looked down at the bravest man I ever knew and said, "Yes, sir."

He would work his way up and down the long rows of corn to try to push the cow toward the road, as I directed his every move. Yet when the cow would see the opened gate and the pasture on the other side she would go crazy. Then Dad went against my directions and just waited at one end of a row of corn, and that old cow headed right towards him. When the cow went past him he just looped a rope over her head and tightened it over her neck.

Once he had her she tamed right down, and he led her to the big barn. She had been eating corn for three or four days, and Dad said she was looking good. But she kept a close eye on my brother and I—and the greatest hunting dog that ever lived.

We decided that we had better try really hard to stay out of trouble because I had a feeling that Dad noticed the way that cow was looking at us. I told my brother that I thought Dad may be getting wise to us. So we helped around the place by feeding the pigs and finding where the hens laid their eggs. And we loved to feed the calves. We even checked in on those monster bulls. We did well for about a month.

Then one delightful day Mom put Anita in her bassinet and placed it out on the front yard, so she could get some fresh air. Old Bob laid right beside the bassinet as he took up his watch. It was something the way that ole mutt loved that little girl.

The more I looked at that bassinet the more it looked like a covered wagon. I remembered my grandfather telling Larry and me about the big wagon his father drove into the Wallowa Valley of Oregon in the 1870s. It looked more and more like that story. All we needed was an ox. First we thought Bob would do, but when we tried to tie him to the bassinet he started to growl at us, so that was out.

I saw it when my brother saw it: the perfect ox. Dad had brought an old billy goat over from the big farm to eat the tall grass and weeds around the house and out in the orchard. What a great ox he would make; we roped him and pulled him over to Anita's bassinet. We tied him to the front of our covered wagon. All the time Bob was growling at us. When I managed to get Bob back away from us, I hit the goat with the loose end of the rope and started off across the front yard.

However, just as we got onto the driveway that would take us out into the big pasture, Dad's pickup truck turned in towards us. The next thing I heard was Mom screaming from the back porch of the house. This all startled the goat, and with the bassinet flying behind him that old goat took off in the wrong direction, toward the open pasture to the south.

Suddenly I realized my baby sister was in that bassinet and she was in real danger. I couldn't hear Mom and Dad screaming at me any more. All I could think of was Anita. In front of us was that big irrigation canal with tall grass growing along its banks. The grass was so thick that the canal couldn't be seen until you were right on top of it. We all knew it was there; however, the goat didn't know, and if he knew he wouldn't know the danger.

Dad had already taken his shirt and boots off to jump into the swift water of the canal.

Just before the goat, bassinet, and Anita went into that canal, I remembered that Bob was running beside the bassinet worrying about his little friend. All the warnings Mom and Dad gave me about that canal came flooding back. That was the one thing my brother and I never went near out of fear.

I couldn't reach that old goat—it was running like a deer. So I screamed the magic word, and within a half dozen strides Bob brought that goat down. Bob lay there across the goat's neck looking him right in the eye.

Mom snatched Anita from the bassinet (she hadn't even woke up) and ran into the house. I was down on my knees holding the goat by the ears helping Bob pin him to the ground. Then Dad's shadow settled over us, and I looked up. He was standing there with his hands on his hips. He looked down at us and said, "Let the goat up."

With the halter rope in his big hands he took the goat back to the orchard and tied him up. The dumb old goat started eating grass again like nothing had happened.

I had never seen my Father without a shirt on, and the scars on his chest and shoulder were something new to me. I learned later in my life that they were from wounds he received in the war. I had never seen so many muscles in my life.

He asked us if we knew why he didn't have his shirt and boots on. We just silently stood there. He said, "Because I was going into that canal after Anita if that goat hadn't stopped."

I knew that the banks of irrigation canals were very steep, and that the water was swift.

Then he went on. "All I may have been able to do was throw Anita up on the bank. I may have died in that swift water. But

I would have done it because you kids and Mom are all I have in this world."

I then realized that I loved this man who went away to war when I was just a baby. We didn't even know him, but we loved him. We started crying and threw ourselves around his mighty legs. Dad held my brother and I for a long time, and then he told us to go take a nap and rest awhile, that he had something he wanted to talk to us about.

We slept until I heard dad's truck start up and head towards the other farm to do the evening milking. We went downstairs, and Mom dished up our supper. She was really quiet as she moved around the kitchen. Then she told us that Grandma and Grandpa were moving back to La Grande next week. She said that they had only moved up to Bainbridge Island so Grandpa could work in the shipyards in Seattle during the war. He was a boilermaker and had put the boilers in a lot of ships during the war. But since the war was over the shipyards were laying people off, so he had decided to retire and come back to their home here in La Grande.

I didn't even know they had a home in La Grande. We were so excited. Grandma was a really good cook, and Grandpa had a lot of really good stories to tell us. What a treat that would be.

We went to bed before Dad got home from the big farm. I lay there for hours wondering what it was Dad wanted to talk to us about. That night I woke up to the quiet sound of Dad's music coming up the stairs. I tiptoed down the stairs and lay in the hall and watched Dad as he sat there in his chair. I couldn't tell if he was sleeping or just had his eyes closed as he listened to his music. And that samurai sword hung there above his head.

Then in almost a whisper I heard his voice. "Johnny come here."

I froze. I didn't know he could tell I was there. At first I just wanted to run back up the stairs. But I walked in by his big chair and stood there. His scriptures were lying in his lap, and his big strong hands lay gently on the arms of his chair. His eyes opened, his head moved ever so slightly, and he looked deep into my eyes.

And he said, "Have you and Larry been siccing Bob on the animals?"

I hung my head and said, "Yes."

Dad folded his hands over his scriptures and said, "We can't have a dog like that on a farm with a bunch of valuable cows that could get hurt. I have to run him off."

When my brother and I lost the best friend we had it almost broke our hearts. Dad bought an old car right after that, and in the rear of this old buggy was a magic place, a rumble seat. Larry and I rode in the back of that old car throughout the farmlands of the Grande Ronde Valley always on the lookout for that magic friend we called Bob.

It was a month later that Dad came home one night and told Mom he had quit his job. I believe Dad had decided that the answers he sought weren't there in the Grande Ronde Valley. He had to go further in his search for explanations to the questions that obsessed him so. It seems that's what war does to people. When the fighting is all over, they spend the rest of their lives looking for answers to the things they have seen and done.

The sudden movement caused the little creatures that I could barely make out above me in the treetops to leap from tree to tree like a bunch of schizophrenic, chattering monkeys. I didn't dare look up to see what they were as I had my eyes trained on the trail ahead looking, ever looking for trip wires. Only an insane madman could hunt another human being, so this place must have been an insane asylum.

The fear of losing my mind was always with me, fear that

I would awake and find myself in a padded cell. I was scared that this world I was in would change before my eyes and the birds and monkeys I heard wouldn't be animals, but lost and caged human beings. Men that shuffled as they walked, looking down at the ground, and when they did look at me there would be no life in their eyes, men that I had seen at American Lake Veterans' Hospital when I pleaded with my brother to go home and swim in Blackjack Creek and renew his soul.

I prayed for the Lord to help conquer my constant fear. I was more afraid of losing my mind than that I was of dying. There were so many things to fear: the viper that was so hard to see as it faded in with the color of green jungle leaves, trip wires, and snipers. I knew that if I ever got out of that madhouse I would always be startled by even the smallest, most harmless water snake, and when I entered a forest I knew I would always watch where I stepped and look up for the Dragon; I wondered if the Dragon was winning.

The M-14 I carried seemed to weigh a ton; every step seemed a little longer. My neck was aching from looking up and down as I looked for danger both on the ground and up in the trees. I cursed every extra round of ammo I carried and even the weight of the extra morphine and medical supplies I had in my rucksack. Was it a sign I was becoming a part of that paranoid insane asylum? But then I thought of the cries of wounded friends because I hadn't packed enough morphine. How many times had I had to stuff a man's dirty T-shirt into a torn and bleeding wound because I didn't have enough sterile dressings? So I stopped cursing the extra weight and kept moving my legs.

It seemed once I reached a certain point of exhaustion (both mental and physical) my mind stopped working, my body just moved on its own, and my fears turned to dreams of home and Blackjack Creek. Man, I was so tired it seemed like the last two years were a lifetime and if I saw one more friend die I would surely lose my mind.

The jungle was so hot it seemed to steam as it tried to steal every ounce of fluid from my body. My Australian jungle hat slipped down over my wet, sweaty forehead and for an instant covered my eyes. My clothes stuck to my body and my socks, boots, and feet seemed to have melted into one wet, hot piece of clay. I feared that if I died in that hellhole I would burn instead of decaying. That jungle seemed hot enough to have been thrown up out of the bowels of hell itself.

I dropped down on the jungle floor to rest. I remember thinking that the insects ruled that insane asylum, and that it wouldn't be long before they took over the rest of the world.

I sat there and rested and tried to see the birds that seemed to be trying to drive us all mad with their crazy songs. I thought back to my teens and Blackjack Creek and all the different birds we had in Washington State. My thoughts shifted to the cool summer nights that I lay on my back in a lonely field near my boyhood home and felt the cool, green grass against my back. I could remember looking up into the sparkling heavens and dreaming my dreams, the dreams of a boy. Then as my mind shifted back to the jungle, the insane asylum, I wondered if the same cool fields would ever be as cool and green and if my dreams would ever be as innocent and hopeful as before. But most of all would I be able to stop hating and being afraid of losing my mind because of the things I'd seen and done? It wouldn't be long before I would feel the cool waters of Blackjack Creek again.

I stood and took the point again and slowly moved forward. I shifted the weight of my pack and cursed at the pain of it grinding into the sore on my spine. My hands slipped on the sweaty stock of my rifle, and I almost lost my grip on it. I cursed the heat of the jungle again, and as I continued forward my mind shifted from the cool, green fields of home and back to what we were about to do.

The little trail we had been following intersected with another trail, only this one was wider. Even the untrained eye could tell which path our prey had taken, and we followed. As we traveled deeper into the jungle we seemed to be leaving the noisy part of the jungle and entering into a silence no could ever believe if told about.

How can I ever tell someone that I've heard the silent sound of death?

Then I heard my grandfather's voice. "Careful, son, the Dragon is near. He is just to the right of you and perched in a tree; be careful, Johnny."

I could make out a clearing just a few feet ahead. I signaled my friends to come up beside me. I told them that he was here and that I was going to quickly step out into the clearing and then step back into the jungle to see if I could get him to move. They didn't like my idea; they wanted to wait, but I wanted to get it over with. I wasn't being brave; I just wanted it to be over.

When they saw they weren't going to change my mind, they took up positions at the edge of the clearing. Tommy stayed right behind me with the idea that if anything moved he would cover me. I had told all of them that I thought he was to the right up in a tree.

I stepped into the clearing and could see it was a bomb crater from another fight, another day. But I wasn't fast enough: as I turned to jump back into the jungle, the Dragon fired and hit me in the leg. Instead of Tommy firing at the muzzle flash in the trees, he jumped to grab me and pull me from harm's way; the Dragon fired again hitting my friend in the chest. With that the whole team opened up on the VC and blew him out of the tree.

My friend died because of me. Why I didn't wait I'll never know. I just couldn't stand that jungle another second; I wanted to see the sky. I wasn't scared of dying, but I didn't want any of my friends to die. Then God had mercy on me, and I blacked out.

When I awoke I was looking into the misty blue eyes of a beautiful woman and could feel the steady drone of airplane engines under my back. I remember asking the owner of those misty blue eyes for something for pain. Then there was more blackness. I came to on an ambulance bus going from an air force base to an army hospital. All I could think of was why Tommy had to die and the fear I felt, the fear of losing my mind, the fear that caused me to step into that clearing.

It's been a long time now, but I still feel the fear sometimes. When I walk into a room I catch myself checking the easiest and fastest way out. I almost always try to sit with my back to the wall. When I walk down a street at night I watch the shadows of the darkened doorways. I always know who's behind me, and I'm always aware of anyone moving to close to me.

Sometimes at night I dream of the Dragon and the mighty fights we had, and the fear seems to stalk me relentlessly. But then the Dragon stops stalking me, I stop stalking him, and my eyes open. And I realize where I'm at home, the world.

EPILOGUE

Moroni 10 Verse 1. Now I Moroni write somewhat as seemeth me good and I write unto my brethren the Lamanites:" I would that they should know that "more than four hundred and twenty years have passed away since the sign was given of the coming of Christ.

Moroni Chapter 10 Verse 2. And I seal up these records, after I have spoken a few words by way of exhortation unto you.

Moroni Chapter 10 Verse 34. And now I bid unto all, farewell. I soon go to rest in the paradise of God until my spirit and body shall again reunite and I am brought forth triumphant through the air, to meet you before the pleasing bar of the great Jehovah, the Eternal Judge of both quick and dead. Amen

ABOUT THE AUTHOR

John Kershaw has what he considers five diplomas; one from Olympic College, one from Central Washington University, one from The Evergreen State College, one from a four-year Boilermaker Apprenticeship and last but not least an Honorable Discharge from the United States Army as a combat medic. John does not want to be remembered as a "man of letters" but as a Sunday School Teacher and when he runs out of the twenty-nine Parables of Jesus Christ, he says he will write his own to get the point across; to help our teenagers to learn how to dream and he refuses to accept the word quit in his vocabulary.